To F... [handwritten]

Enjoy the Game [handwritten]

THE WOMAN GOLFER

A BEGINNER'S GUIDE

SECOND EDITION

Written by
Mary Jane Dillon
Custis N. Proctor

Like We do! [handwritten]

Foreword by
Donna White

Illustrations by
Frank R. DeDeo

Christmas 1998 [handwritten]

ISBN: 0-9650385-0-5

Additional copies of this book may be ordered from:
Severn Group
3149 N. Ponce de Leon Blvd.
St. Augustine, FL 32084

Foreword

by
Donna White
Former LPGA Tour Winner
Director of Golf, The Wellington Club, Wellington, Florida

I have often thought that the most difficult part of golf is getting started. Most new golfers have never before set foot on a golf course. The equipment is new, the people are different, and everything feels strange. A professional woman in a business setting may find herself in atmosphere where everyone plays golf. Then she's the one who sits by the pool at corporate outings and misses all the "networking."

The first task facing a beginning golfer is to overcome the feelings of uncertainty and awkwardness that go along with getting involved in any new activity. In the course of a lesson, the grip, the stance, and the swing can be taught; however, it's hard to find the time to tell a student everything she needs to know to make her feel ready to go out on the course.

The Woman Golfer: A Beginner's Guide provides a useful introduction to the game. It does not take the place of a professional teacher; rather, it helps the pro to do his or her job. It gives the student essential information in preparation for the "first tee jitters!" Most important, reading this book will help the beginning golfer feel more at ease on the course.

Contents

Introduction

*A*lthough there have been in the past few years a great
many books written upon golf, detailing how to play the
game, and the things one should do and likewise leave
undone, there has never been a book which presented the Royal
and Ancient game to the feminine inquiring mind and from a
woman's standpoint. It is my purpose and desire to supply this
deficiency, so far as I may be able to do so, in the chapters that
make up this book. . . No matter how valuable to a man the
present text-books of the game may be, I have found that there
were many points about the best of them which were wholly
incomprehensible to a woman. That this is quite to be expected
is natural, for how can a man understand the ways and moods
and means which must be taken into consideration when a
woman prepares to golf?
Genevieve Hecker, 1902
National Woman Golf Champion 1901-02; 1902-03

These words were written almost a century ago. Genevieve Hecker, then the National Woman Golf Champion, wrote the first book about golf for women at the turn of the century. She said then that the number of serious women golfers at the time warranted the publication of a book solely for women on the subject of golf.

If that were so then, how much more important is it today! There are an estimated 30 million golfers in the U.S. today, and an additional 20 million are expected by the year 2000, 40% of whom will be women, according to the National Golf Foundation.

Young women are being introduced to golf as an athletic option in high school and college. Career women are finding golf can be a useful adjunct to a business career. And golf continues to be a popular recreational activity for women in their leisure hours.

But regardless of age, circumstance, or reason for being interested in the sport, all new women golfers need a place from which to begin. This is the place.

The following chapters have been written to introduce women to the game of golf. Among subjects covered are the rules of the game, golf etiquette, equipment, language, handicapping, scoring, and how to play an average hole. In short, this book will help you feel at home when you first venture out onto a golf course.

Certain topics are not covered: specifically, how to hold or swing a club. This instruction is best obtained through direct contact with a professional golf instructor. But if the lessons of this book are mastered in advance of, or along with, the lessons taught by a "pro" on the driving range, the new golfer will be well on her way to becoming a player who is not only competent but also comfortable on the course.

Why golf?

Golfers can give you a variety of answers to this question. Among some of the most frequently heard are the following.

- Golf is a lifetime sport. You may start as a teenager or younger and continue to enjoy the game into your eighties and nineties.

- Golf is played in some of the most beautiful surroundings nature has to offer. Courses are located near the seashore, in the mountains, and are, almost without exception, beautiful to behold. While playing golf, you will also enjoy the sight of rare birds flying overhead, fish jumping in the water, flowers blooming, and woods animals scurrying for cover.
- Golf can be enjoyed alone or as a social activity. On the course you will see many solitary golfers, some of whom are intently practicing their game, while others are unwinding with a relaxing round in the late afternoon.
- Golf is also a wonderful group activity, especially because you can play golf with any other golfer. It is not necessary that you be as good as they are, nor that they be as skilled as you. The handicap system (described in a later chapter) puts all players on an equal level. As a result, you can enjoy playing golf with your best friend, a business associate, your husband, or your in-laws. You can enjoy golf with your children and other family members. And remember, golf is not just for now, but for always.

"Beginner's Luck"

One concluding thought … If the game of golf attracts you and you like your first encounters with the sport, you may be embarked on a life-changing adventure. Few golfers are neutral about the game. Most are crazy about it and relish the hours of fun, challenge, and camaraderie which golf offers. So if you're a beginner — lucky you! You're about to make the discovery of a lifetime!

Where it all Began

The Origins of Golf

There has been much speculation as to where and how the game of golf began. To a great extent, it depends upon how the game is defined, since there are records of games which used clubs and balls being played throughout history.

Fourteenth century German paintings show shepherds striking rocks with sticks, perhaps to take advantage of a 1338 hunting law, which specified that grazing rights could be extended into the forest as far as a pebble could be hit with a single stroke.

Most would agree, however, that Scotland deserves credit for developing the game of golf as we know it today — played with a variety of clubs, over an extended area, with the object of hitting a ball into a hole.

The first written record of golf in Scotland was James I's edict of 1457. This declared that golf was illegal because it interfered with the compulsory archery practice, deemed necessary to ensure national security.

While James I banned golf in the mid-fifteenth century, another royal James (VI of Scotland and I of England) is credited with introducing the game in England and promoting its popularity to a level that has not diminished in modern times.

The First "Courses"

The game of golf was first played on the Scottish coast in areas known as "links" because they linked the farmland to the sea. As golf became more popular, it was played on fields called "commons," or public grounds. Paintings from the 19th century show both men and women dressed in tailored red jackets, the color being a safety precaution intended to alert others that players were striking balls on the commons.

Early golf courses consisted of three, seven, or any number of holes. The first St. Andrews course consisted of 11 holes out and 11 back. During these times, ladies had their own courses, which were shorter.

The first records of a golf club being formed was in Edinburgh in 1744. Today, this is the noted course at Muirfield. St. Andrews put in an appearance ten years later, and subsequently was named the Royal and Ancient Society.

The first course on the continent was established in 1856 at Pau in France, where women had their own nine-hole course as early as 1880. The Calcutta Club, established in India in 1829, was the first golf club formed outside of England.

Golf first appeared on American shores along the Carolina and Georgia coasts, no doubt introduced by the large number of Scottish settlers in those regions. The first actual golf club in America was established in Yonkers, New York, around 1888 by John Reid, a transplanted Scotsman.

Equipment

The early golf set consisted of four or five woods and perhaps one or, at most, two iron clubs. Shafts made of hazel or ash made the clubs whippy, and players took long backswings to control direction and distance. Around the middle of the last century, hickory from the Carolinas and Tennessee was shipped to England. This replaced ash, and became the standard club shaft until the mid 1930's, when it gave way to steel.

Golf bags were a fairly recent invention, coming into use at the turn of the century. Caddies, who appeared on the links in the late nineteenth century, carried clubs by hand.

The first golf balls were made of leather stuffed with feathers or horse hair. Construction of these balls was time-consuming and expensive. In a 10-hour work day, a ballmaker could produce only four to five feather balls. The gutta-percha ball was introduced around 1850. This ball could be manufactured in molds, and it made golf much more affordable.

The third step in ball evolution was the development of the Haskell in 1899. It was wound rubber with a hard exterior. Suddenly, players were hitting the ball much farther, and many of the old courses were either made longer or abandoned.

A later modification of the Haskell was a new ball covering made of balata. This resulted in a softer ball, allowing the padding of the club's grip to be reduced and permitting a change in the way in which the club was held. The new way of gripping the club, which is still in use today, ultimately became known as the Vardon grip. It was named for Harry Vardon, the most famous golfer of the day.

Gals In Golf

*N*ever before in all my experience have I seen such universal grit, sand, or what I belive you call "nerve" as is displayed by every woman golfer in America.

Rhona Adair, 1905 English Open Champion (3 years) and Irish Open Champion (5)

Don't ever think that women are latecomers to the game of golf. Women have been involved since the earliest days of the sport! As early as 1567, Mary Queen of Scots was subjected to severe criticism for playing golf only a few days after the death of her husband!

13

During the second half of the nineteenth century, women had organized their own golf clubs. The courses were shorter than those played by men, and there were significant differences in the way the game was played.

The clothes of the era imposed severe restrictions on movement, and it was considered to be unladylike to raise the club above shoulder height. Nonetheless, a review of art works of the 19th century reveals a number of impressive portrayals of dignified and graceful lady golfers.

Turning Point

The year 1893 marked a turning point in the history of women's golf. In England, the Ladies' Golf Union was formed. This group was inspired by its honorary secretary, Issette Pearson, runner-up to Lady Margaret Scott in the first British Ladies' Amateur Championship of the same year. Indeed, Lady Scott won the first three LGU tournaments with scores in the 80's, an impressive accomplishment when you consider that the American, Mrs. Charles Brown, won the first U.S. Golf Association competition in 1895 with a score of 132, and that was on nine holes! Among other famous names associated with the LGU was that of Lady Nancy Astor, the first woman to take a seat in Parliament.

Across the Atlantic and also in 1893, American wives of the members of the Shinnecock Hills Club in New York persuaded their husbands to build them their own separate nine-hole course. This solution to the problem of gaining access to men's golf courses became a model for women golfers. In situations where men refused to allow women on the established course, women created their own. By 1894, women had established their own club, as well as a seven-hole course, in Morristown, New Jersey.

Early Winners

In the following decades, women became increasingly active on the links. Among the notable female players was Charlotte Cecilia Pitcairn Leitch. In 1908, at the tender age of 17, she reached the semifinals of the British Ladies' Amateur. Shortening her name to Cecil Leitch in 1914, she continued to collect trophies in the early years of this century, winning 12 titles in Britain, France, and Canada. Leitch was the pre-eminent British player until supplanted by Joyce Wethered. Wethered took eight titles in four years, retiring from competion in 1925. A comeback four years later, resulted in her fourth British Ladies' Amateur title, won at St. Andrews. A principal rival in that final was a cross-Atlantic champion, the American, Glenna Collett. Collett took the American Women's Amateur Championship six times.

The spirited competition between American and British women golfers has been underway since the turn of the century. An American team first traveled to Britain in 1905 to play in the British Ladies' Amateur. Also of interest is the fact that the first international women's trophy was donated by two American sisters. Harriot and Margaret Curtis, who played in the 1905 event, donated the Curtis Cup and saw Americans win the first Cup match in 1932. The American women remained undefeated until the British won in 1952. Americans regained dominance shortly after, losing to the British subsequently only in 1956, 1986, and 1988.

Professional Golf

It was not until well after the Second World War that women's golf was transformed from an amateur to a professional sport. The Ladies' Professional Golf Association (LPGA) was formed in 1949, but for many years tournaments were few, and prize money was negligible compared to that offered to male players.

The first women professional golfers and leaders in the new LPGA were Patty Berg and Mildred Didrikson Zaharias. "Babe" Zaharias, as she was called, had been a track star in her youth, and took up golf toward mid-life. When ex-wrestler George Zaharias proposed to Babe, she responded that she wouldn't marry a man who couldn't hit the ball as far as she could. Zaharias took Babe's driver and put the ball twenty yards past hers. He never picked up a club again. She, on the other hand, went on to win 17 tournaments in 1946 alone, and was a dominant force in the early days of the LPGA.

In her book, *The Education of a Woman Golfer,* LPGA pro Nancy Lopez says that it was not until the 1940's that women's professional golf began to make headway. But even by 1948, there

15

were only nine tournaments, and Babe, the leading money winner, took home only $3,400 in prize money. Five years later Louise Suggs won $20,000. In 1963, Mickey Wright claimed the position of dominant player; there were 28 tournaments that year, and Mickey took in $30,000 in official winnings.

During the 1970's, when Nancy Lopez was at the peak of her career, women's professional golf was well established both in prize money and media attention. In her rookie year of 1978, Nancy won $200,000, and others, such as Kathy Whitworth and Carol Mann, were accumulating hundreds of thousands of dollars in prize money winnings.

In later decades, television coverage and annual prize dollars in the millions became commonplace. Curiously, in Britain, the professional game was not established until 1979, and failed to attract a significant public following. Only in recent years has a European tour become a feature of the sports world. After 70 years of the Ryder Cup, women professional golfers could claim an equivalent competition. In 1990, the Solheim Cup was won by the American team by a margin of 11 1/2 to 4 1/4.

Women in Golf Today

Not surprisingly, amateur women's involvement in the game of golf also expanded dramatically in recent years. The National Golf Foundation reports a 9.7% annual growth rate among women golfers between 1986 and 1992, outdistancing the growth among male players. Indeed, about 40% of all new players since 1990 have been women, many of whom were also involved in full-time careers. Half of women golfing today are reported to be in professional, managerial and administratrive positions.

Starting Right

A *beginner was anxiously inquiring of a dour plain-spoken old professional how long it took a man to become a great golfer. "Well," said the old fellow slowly, "If your father and your grandfather and his father before him were muckle good golfers, and you began as a little child, by the time you were grown up you should play pretty fair."*

Quoted in "Golf for Women," 1904

If, ultimately, you would like to play well, then start well! Playing well is based on two fundamentals:

    A. Instruction
    B. Practice

Instruction

A proper start begins with proper instruction. Better to begin right than to take amateur advice and hack around the course. It is much harder to correct a wrong grip, wrong stance, and wrong swing than it is to begin properly.

17

Nowhere in this publication will you be told how to swing a golf club. There are hundreds of books that try to do just that, notwithstanding the fact that a golfer may be short, tall, narrow, wide, agile, stiff, right-handed, or left-handed. Of course, golfers are all of the above and in various combinations. It would take a multi-volume encyclopedia to provide all of these new golfers with the proper beginning instruction.

To get started right, see your professional, and do it now!

Among the options open to you are individual lessons, group lessons, golf schools, and clinics. Most likely, you will find that a series of lessons will offer a saving. At almost any club, a professional golf instructor will be glad to arrange a lesson time. If a pro is specifically recommended, then contact him or her as the case may be. Yes, there are many more lady PGA instructors than you might think!

The Lesson

The call you make to the pro will result in a time, date, and place for your lesson. Please be on time! If you have no clubs, don't worry about that. Your instructor can provide clubs which are just right for you. He or she can also advise you as to what length, weight, and loft are best suited to your physical makeup before you invest in equipment.

One thing to remember: this is a golf lesson, not a garden party. Wear a loose shirt with a collar, then shorts, slacks or a short skirt. Just be comfortable. Sport shoes with good support are OK, assuming you have not yet purchased golf shoes.

There is no reason to feel intimidated during a lesson. The only person on the 250-acre golf course that is the least bit interested in your swing, stance, dress, etc. is the instructor!

Practice

Almost all golf courses have areas which are set aside for practice. There is most often a driving range and also a practice putting green. Many courses have a special green, where you can practice sand shots as well as chipping and pitching.

In any sport except bungee jumping, a lot more time is devoted to practice than playing. A professional sports team practices all week for just a few hours in the spotlight. As a beginner, you should put in the time necessary to help you correct faults and improve technique. Do this, and the results will come through ten-fold on the course.

What to Practice

Putting	Pitch & Chip	Irons	Woods
40%	20%	15%	25%

The table above shows the amount of time you spend using specific clubs on the course. Thus, it follows that you should allocate the same percentage of your practice time to each shot.

Putting and Chipping

A two-foot putt counts just the same on the score card as a 250-yard drive, and around the green is where you can save the strokes. With a little finesse and a lot of practice, women can out-putt, out-chip, and out-pitch most of the guys on the course. For in this area, strength is not a factor!

The putter hears his own drummer. It doesn't look like other clubs, lie like other clubs, or even feel like other clubs. Take time to select your putter, and try out a number of models until you come across that special instrument that feels right and looks right, for you will be looking at it a lot! Practice long putts, medium putts, and those short putts, which are sometimes referred to as "tap-ins." You can putt on the practice green, putt at home on the carpet, and you can even practice your putting stroke without a putter in hand.

After a few rounds and some professional lessons, you will know just where you need practice. Your instructor will also tell you in what areas you need to work, and a good teacher will tell you, in specific terms, just how to go about that practice.

A last reminder: refer to the table above to bring to mind the relative benefit to your game of slamming out drives on the range as compared to the crick-in-the-neck accomplishment of accurate chipping and putting.

"Golfese"
If You Play, Speak the Language

*T*he most useful word in the golfer's vocabulary — or at least the one which will describe the golfer's efforts at first, most frequently, I am afraid — is "foozle," which can be applied to any stroke which does not result the way the player intended it to do."
Genevieve Hecker, 1904

Ace   Hole in one; very rare other than on a par three hole.

Albatross   Three under par; the same as a double eagle.

Away	Describes the player who is farthest from the pin.
Ball Mark	An indentation in the grass, which was made by a ball landing on the green.
Birdie	One shot under par, i.e. a score of three on a four-par hole.
Blast	A shot from a sand bunker.
Blind Green	A green that cannot be seen from the tee box.
Bogie	One shot over par, i.e. a score of five on a four-par hole. A double bogie on a par four would be a six.
Break	The slant of the green between the ball and the hole is called a break; it can be to the right or the left.
Bump and Run	A long punch shot used to hit short of the green and roll on.
Bunker	A hazard consisting of a prepared area of ground, often a hollow, from which grass has been removed and replaced with sand or a similar substance.
Carry	The distance the ball moves through the air before landing.
Chip	An approach shot used when the ball is close to the green. It has more roll and less loft than a pitch shot.
Cleats	Spikes on golf shoes which provide traction.
Compression	The hardness rating on a golf ball. The softest is 80, the middle is 90; 100 is the hardest, and is used by the very low handicapper.
"Corn" or "Tulies"	Southern expressions referring to the area of the course known as the "rough."

Dimples	Indentations on golf balls, which give loft and direction.
Distance Markers	Stakes, trees, shrubs, or in-ground concrete blocks, which mark the distance to the center of the green, usually placed at 200, 150, and 100 yards.
Divot	A piece of turf which is cut out by the club when it is stroked through the ball.
Dogleg	A hole in which the fairway curves sharply to the left or the right.
Dormie	Describes the following situation: you have played six holes out of nine. You are three holes down to your opponent with three left to play. You have the chance to tie, but can't win. You are dormie.
Draw	A shot curving to the left.
Drive	Initial shot from the tee box with persimmon or metal wood.
Duck Hook	A shot that takes a sharp left turn.
Eagle	Two under par, i.e. a score of three on a par five.
Fade	A shot that falls off to the right.
Fairway	The stretch of short grass that lies between the tee and the green.
Fat Shot	Hitting the ground before the ball; a mishit.
Flop Shot	A high approach shot landing with little roll.
Flyer	A high, sailing ball, often resulting from a shot hit from the rough.
"Fore!"	Loud shout used to alert others on the course that a struck ball may endanger another player.

Fringe	The short grass, encircling but not part of the green. May also be called "frog hair."
Gimme	A very close putt that is conceded.
Grain	Inclination of blades of grass on the green.
Green	Putting surface where the pin is placed.
Ground (verb)	To rest the club head on the ground behind the ball when lining up a shot.
Hazard	Penalty area marked by stakes, such as water, marshes, etc.
Hardpan	Hard ground surface with little or no grass.
Honor	The person who wins the previous hole has the *honor* of hitting the first shot on the succeeding tee.
Hook	A shot going sharply left.
Knockdown	A low hit shot, often used to avoid overhead limbs or high winds.
Lie	The position of the ball on the course.
Match Play	Hole by hole play against opponent(s).
Medal Play	Total 18-hole score against opponent(s).
Mulligan	One extra shot on the first tee; optional with group of players, not encouraged.
"On the Screws"	Describes a solid, long hit.
Out	Describes the player who is farthest from hole; same as "away."
Out-of-Bounds "O.B."	The area where play is prohibited, generally marked by stakes or lines drawn on the ground.

Pin	Flagstick.
Pin High	Describes a ball hit onto or near the green which is directly in line with the pin.
Plugged	Ball is deep in the ground with only the top showing.
Putt	Rolling shot on the green.
Pitch	Lofted approach shot with less roll than a chip.
Pull	A shot moving to your left.
Push	A shot moving to your right.
Rough	The area bordering the fairway, un-maintained terrain, woods, high grass, etc.
Sandie	Hitting from a sand bunker to the green and into the hole in two strokes.
Sandbagger	A critical term which describes a player who is carrying a higher handicap than is appropriate for his level of play.
Shank	A shot which is mis-hit off the shank of the club, resulting in the ball's scooting to the right.
Skied-Shot	A high-flying and short shot, *pronounced "sky-ed."*
Skull Shot	A shot which is hit accidentally with the bottom blade of the club, producing a rolling, bumping shot.
Slice	A sailing shot that goes off to the right.
Snake	A very long putt that goes in the cup.
Stance	Body position taken in preparing to swing.
Stroke	Any swing hitting or intending to hit the ball.
Stymie	Line of play blocked by object, tree, rock; (stymied).

Tee Box	Driving area with tee markers. Red tee markers are for ladies; white tees are the men's regular tees; blue or gold tees are men's championship tees. Other colors may be used to designate tees for senior players.
Tee Time	The time reserved for you to begin your game.
Top (verb)	Hitting high up on the ball, sending it rolling.
Unplayable	Lie of ball makes swing impossible; the ball may be moved with a penalty stroke.
Up	As in, "Who's Up?" "Whose turn is it to hit?"
Whiff	A swing (stroke) that misses the ball.
Wind Cheater	Low flying ball used against the wind.
Worm Burner	Hard, bouncing mishit which results in the ball rolling along the ground.

Your Golf Tools

Basic Equipment

As a beginner, while you are taking lessons and practicing, a full set of clubs is not absolutely required. Once you determine that this is a game for you, then is the time to invest in clubs. Initially, a light canvass or nylon golf bag is fine. These generally provide one or two pockets for balls and a larger pocket, which will accommodate a rain suit, head cover, and miscellaneous items such as bug spray and gloves.

Shoes

There are many styles and colors of golf shoes from which to choose. Shoes can be expensive; however, your first pair does not have to be the top-of-the-line. Later, as you get into the game, you will want to invest in good quality shoes. Waterproof shoes are recommended if you live in an area which gets a lot of rain. If at all possible, let your golf professional assist you with the selection and the fitting. If your size is not in stock, shoes can be ordered for you. White, street-style shoes are the most popular because they go well with almost any outfit. In selecting a golf shoe, please remember that comfort and support are more important than style.

Clubs

According to the rules, you may carry less but not more than 14 clubs. Up until this century, individual clubs were differentiated by name rather than by number. There were bulger drivers, spoons (later to be three-woods) cleeks, niblicks, mashies, and diggers. Today's numbering of clubs is simpler, but somehow don't seem to give the clubs quite as much personality!

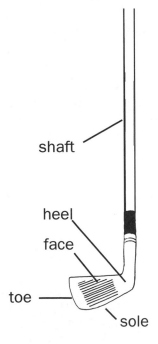

shaft

heel

face

toe

sole

Irons: In the sketch on the left, you will note the correct nomenclature of a club. The "irons," as they are called, although they are made of steel, are numbered one through nine. The numbers refer to the loft or tilt of the club head, which ranges from the one iron, having the least loft, and gradually increases to the nine iron and the wedges, which have the most loft. You seldom see a one, two, or three iron in a lady's bag. They are difficult to master, and one of the wood clubs will do the job better with far less chance of resulting in a bad shot.

27

The heads of your irons are made of steel. They may be cast, that is made from liquid steel and poured in a mold. Or, they may be forged into the desired shape. As a matter of choice, most professionals use the forged product, while amateurs prefer the more forgiving cast club head.

Among the most frequently used irons are the wedges. These include many different styles and lofts. Sand wedges are just what they say they are: a club to hit the ball from the sand in the bunker. The pitching wedge is used to pitch the ball with a lot of loft (height). It is also used by the average female from a distance of 40 yards or less into the green. Both clubs are handy for hitting over objects such as bunkers or mounds.

Woods: All clubs were originally wooden shafted. This gave way to steel, which, along with graphite, are the shafts you see today. Your wooden clubs are your distance clubs; they're called "woods," even though some have steel or composite heads. The driver, or one wood, has so little loft that it is used with a wooden peg, or tee, to raise the height of the ball.

Buying Clubs

Here, be selective and careful. Your clubs will be your tools for the game. With proper selection and fit, you will be together a long time. When not in play, they are usually close behind you in your car's trunk. Prior to being placed there, they were cleaned by you or a bag boy. In spite of all the modern alloys, they will still rust, and the grooves will accumulate grit and dirt. If you live in a warm climate, remember that the extreme heat in a car's trunk can cause damage. Take good care of them!

Club Features

In selecting your own set of clubs, it is recommended that you have a professional golfer help you. Clubs are a significant investment, and there are a number of features to consider in choosing a set which will help you play your best game. He or she will cover many of the following points:

- **Quality** Let your budget guide you.
- **Length** This is determined by your build, stance, and posture.
- **Grip** Choose what's comfortable and what you like.
- **Flex** Shafts come with a "regular" or a "stiff" flex. This is

simply the amount of whip or bend in the shaft. There are also seniors' and ladies' flex grades, which give impetus to the less forceful swing. Women golfers generally prefer more flex in the shafts.

- **Lie** The set of the base of the club head to the ground.
- **Look** The look and design of the club head vary greatly among the various manufacturers. Choose what appeals to you.

Balls

Modern-day balls come in two classifications: three and two-piece balls. Three-piece balls consist of a hard or liquid inner-core, a wrapping, and generally a balata outer cover.

Three-piece ball features:
- Provide a high rate of spin.
- Are easily damaged or cut by the club head.
- Generally are of high compression and are preferred by most professionals and better amateur players.

Two-piece ball features:
- Are very durable, more so than a balata ball.
- Are less expensive that a balata ball.
- Are the choice of amateur players.

The term "compression" is used to describe the hardness of the ball.

Grade 100 is very hard, and is used by professional golfers and amateurs with very low handicaps.

Grade 90 is the most popular, and is a small degree softer than the above.

Grade 80 is the favorite of many lady players, whose swings are slower-paced than those of men.

One more note on the subject of balls. You will see many colored balls, pink, blue, and red, advertised as "ladies'" golf balls. From the point of view of good taste, stick to white, and save the colors for Easter eggs!

What To Wear

" The debate as to whether corsets should be worn or not worn on the links is really unimportant, for in these days no woman who is sufficiently up-to-date and athletic to play golf, is far enough behind the times to lace."

Caroline Manice, 1902

A heavy pair of boots, any kind of a short skirt, and a waist which leaves one free for a good full swing are all that are necessary, and they are alike the world over.

**Rhona Adair, 1905; English Open Champion (3 years)
Irish Open Champion (5 years)**

The debate over what to wear for golf is not new, and women's concern for their appearance is no less evident on the course than in other settings. This is particularly true of the beginning golfer.

There may be a temptation to rush out to buy new clothes, emblazoned with colorful golfing symbols such as tees, pins, and balls. While such items may look great in the pro shop, hold off purchasing them until your game has progressed to the point at which you can risk calling more attention to your wardrobe than to your strokes.

Dress Smart

The critical elements in golf attire are comfort and suitability. Most golf clubs, both private and semi-private courses, have a dress code. While few clubs still require that women wear golf skirts, most specify that shirts must have a collar, and few permit T-shirts or denim in any form. Shorts are fine, but should be close to knee-length.

A good rule of thumb is to start with conservative clothing. A good working wardrobe is khaki, navy, and/or black shorts or slacks, depending on the weather in the area where you play, with contrasting colored shirts with a collar. Shorts or slacks can be made of any material (other than denim), but shirts should be made of a knit fabric to allow for freedom of movement.

Outer Wear

For cool weather, cotton or light wool sweaters offer good protection. A windbreaker can be added as needed. Many of these items are sold in pro shops and golf specialty stores, and include a golfing logo. Be sure to choose a size that does not restrict your movements — even if it is a size larger than you would normally wear!

On Top

Most women have to wear some form of head gear to keep their hair out of their eyes and to provide protection from the sun. Depending on your hair cut and what you find comfortable, you may choose from a visor, baseball-style cap, or a man's-style straw hat. Any of the above are suitable. Remember, the average time for an 18-hole round is four hours. Purchase a hat that will be comfortable for the duration, and make sure it fits well enough so that it will not blow off in the wind.

In Sum

In conclusion, a successful golf outfit is one which is so appropriate and and so comfortable that you do not have to think about it all. Nearly a century ago, Frances Griscom, the Merion Cricket Club champion in 1900, summed it up nicely: "I do not believe when a woman gets in a game of golf that she ever thinks twice about her appearance. The game simply takes her out of herself. If it does not, she is not a good player."

When and Where to Play

*W*hen women in America first began to play golf,
they were allowed at many of the big clubs to use
the links only at certain hours on certain days
when it was thought that their presence would not
incommode the Lords of Creation.
Genevieve Hecker, 1904

There are basically four types of golf facilities: private clubs, semi-private clubs, public courses, and golf resorts.

Private Clubs

Private courses are not impregnable fortresses. You may play with a member or often on your own, if you are sponsored by a member. Occasionally, a visit during mid-week and a chat with the pro will get you on a private course, assuming you are a member of an out-of-town club. It is worth a try.

Semi-Private Clubs

Semi-private clubs are open to non-members at specified

times. If a convenient tee time is available on the day you wish to play, you are most welcome.

Public Courses

Public courses are just that — open to the public. These courses may be crowded, so be sure to phone ahead to reserve a tee time two to three days in advance if possible. If you are playing alone or with one partner, you may be paired with other players.

Golf Resorts

There are a lot of them, and they can be fun — by yourself or with a partner. Be sure to check rates. Off-season offers great bargains. The reduction can be as much as 50%, so these times are worth waiting for.

If you love the game, a golf resort offers a great vacation for the whole family. Write the Chamber of Commerce in the area you wish to visit. The abundance of reply mail will give you a wide range of choices among accommodations, courses, and rates.

Other Options

Par three courses are great places for beginners to play. These courses are made up of short holes, which range in length from 100 - 200 yards. Many are lighted for night play.

An executive course is one level up from a par three. These courses include some par four holes, but take less time to play than a regulation 18 holes.

Also remember that you do not have to play a full 18 holes when you first start the game. Many beginners will start by playing nine holes. If space is available on your course, you can play the front nine one day and the back nine another. Many courses offer a "twilight" rate for late afternoon play.

Yet another choice is a driving range. These are listed in the Yellow Pages of your phone book, and you don't have to reserve a tee time to take advantage of them. Rental clubs are often available, and some ranges also offer practice putting greens as well as areas where you can practice chipping, pitching, and bunker shots.

Rules to Know

*T*he first thing to do, if one wishes to play golf, is to read *some good book on the game, in order to acquire a general understanding of what one is trying to do.*
Genevieve Hecker, 1904

A booklet entitled, *The Rules of Golf* is published annually by the United States Golf Association. All players should be familiar with these rules, and it is even advisable to carry a rule book with you in your golf bag. To get you started, however, the rules which are most important for you to know are summarized in this chapter. If at any time in your play, you are in doubt about a rule and you don't have a rule book handy, rely on the following maxim:

Play it where it lies and do what is fair!

On the Tee

At the beginning of each hole, the ball must be placed between the two tee markers. The ball may be placed up to two club lengths behind the tee markers, but never in front of them.

The tee may be used to raise your ball only on the teeing ground. If the ball falls off the tee, you may replace it without a penalty. If you swing at the ball and cause it to roll off the tee, you must count the swing as a stroke and play the ball from where it lies on the teeing ground.

You are allowed to take a practice swing; however, if you swing at the ball and miss it, this is called a whiff and counts as a stroke.

On the Fairway

While you are playing the hole, you are not allowed to touch or move the ball. The ball must be played as it lies except in the special circumstances listed below.

If necessary, you may lift your ball in order to identify it. Also, if necessary, you may clean the surface of the ball in order to read the mark.

If you mistake your ball for someone else's, inform your partners and return to the place from which you hit the wrong ball. You incur a two-stroke penalty for hitting the wrong ball.

If your ball is lost or out-of-bounds, return to the place from where you hit your last shot and continue the play. Add to your score the shot you hit out-of-bounds *and* a one stroke penalty.

If your ball cannot be hit where it lies, as in the case where it is resting against a tree or under a bush, you may do one of the following:

- drop the ball within two club lengths of its current position, but not closer to the hole.
- play the ball from where you hit your last shot.
- play the ball from any point between where you hit the original shot and its current position, but no nearer to the hole.

Whichever you choose, you must take a penalty stroke.

In a Hazard

If your ball lands in a water hazard, you have a choice of actions. First, you must determine if you have landed in a regular water hazard or a lateral water hazard. Regular water hazards are generally marked with yellow stakes and are located as an obstacle between the fairway and the green. Lateral water hazard are defined with red stakes and are generally located to the side of the fairway.

If you land in a *regular* water hazard and the ball is not playable, you may:

- mark the point at which the ball entered the hazard and hit you next shot from behind that point; or,
- play another shot from where you hit your last shot.
  In either case, you must count the stroke you hit into the water, and add a penalty stroke to your score.

If you land in a *lateral* water hazard and the ball is not playable, you may:

- hit a new ball from within two club lengths of where your ball entered the hazard, but no nearer the hole; or,
- hit a new ball from the opposite side of the hazard. You may not position the ball any closer to the hole than the point at which your ball entered the water.

In either case, you must count the shot you hit into the water and add a penalty stroke to your score.

Of course, water is not the only hazard you will encounter on the course. There are also marshes, ditches, mud and other unsavory places. And, on almost every hole, you will face up to a sand hazard.

In a sand hazard, you may not ground your club. You may take a practice swing outside the hazard, but once you address the ball in the hazard, your club may not touch the sand.

You may move your ball without a penalty in the following situations:

- your ball lands in standing water that is not marked as a hazard.
- your ball lands in an area of the course which is under repair.
- an object such as a rope, hose, or yardage stick interferes with your shot.
- your ball lands on or next to a cart path, bench, tee sign, or ball washer.

- your ball lands in a hole made by an animal.

The correct manner of moving your ball is to stand facing the hole, extend your arm, and drop the ball to your side. You may not move the ball closer to the hole.

On the Green

You may repair ball marks, remove branches, leaves, or grass in the line of your putt, and mark your ball with a ball marker.

You may lift and clean your ball, but be sure to replace it in the spot in which it landed.

You incur a two-stroke penalty if you are putting on the green and your ball hits the flagstick. If, however, the pin is struck by a ball which is putted from off the green, there is no penalty.

In a Match

The following rules are particularly important if you are playing a match or a tournament. While you may be playing for fun, never underestimate how seriously your opponents may feel about the final score! So. . .

Don't Practice Where You Shouldn't. In match or stroke competition, there can be no practice shots taken on the course between holes or anywhere else. It is permissible to chip or putt only on the green of a completed hole and provided it does not interfere with play.

Don't Ask For or Give Advice. In a match, you may only exchange advice with your partner or your caddy. You cannot give or receive advice from your opponent, e.g. choice of club, direction of wind, etc.

Whose Ball? Every brand of ball is numbered; however, in a match it is a good idea to mark your ball with a personal identification since another player may be using the same make and number of ball. If you cannot identify your ball because it is stuck face down in the fairway or rough, you may lift it, clean it if necessary, and replace it. Be sure to tell your opponents what you are doing. A ball may not be lifted, however, even to identify it, if it has landed in a hazard.

Interference! In taking your stance, always remember that you are not permitted to move limbs or pat down brush, grass, or sand that may be in your way. The only movement of such objects may occur in the process of taking your swing.

Second Hit. It is fairly common that in striking your ball a mis-hit will cause the club head to rise faster than the ball, causing it to strike the ball a second time. In this event, you are charged two strokes rather than one.

Ball Hits Ball. Be sure to ask your opponent to mark his ball on the green if it is close to the line of your putt. In the event your ball strikes another ball at rest on the green, you incur a two-stroke penalty!

Lift and Clean. When on the putting green, you may legally lift and clean your ball prior to putting. Before picking up the ball, be sure and mark it by placing a small coin or ball marker behind it. Then lift, clean, replace it and remove the ball marker.

The Cliff Hanger. Should your ball stop on the very edge of the cup and there is some possibility it will fall in of its own accord, you may wait ten seconds for it to drop. After that time, you must tap it in and count the stroke.

The Leaner. With the flagstick in certain positions, the ball may end up wedged between the rim of the cup and the stick. In this event, you may remove the stick from the hole. If the ball falls in, you score! If not, you need another stroke to hole out.

The Gimme. Even if your ball is nudging the edge of the cup, there are no gimmes in stroke play. In match play, your opponent has the option of giving you the short putt.

Who's Out There

The Parking Lot and Bag Drop

Arriving at an unfamiliar club can be a little confusing. Should there be a sign near the entrance that says "Bag Drop," stop there to unload your clubs before proceeding to the parking lot.

In some instances, there is no bag drop, so go directly to the parking area. A bag boy will bring a cart to your car and help you unload your clubs. These bag boys (by the way, they are not all boys!) are also there to clean your clubs at the end of a round and to place them in the trunk. Tipping of $1 or $2 is encouraged at the beginning and/or end of the round.

The Pro Shop

Your next stop will be the pro shop, where you register for play and pay your green and cart fees. Here, you will find the **head professional**, who manages the shop and supervises the overall operation of the facility.

He or she may have one or two **assistant pros**. They check in the guests, arrange tee times, manage inventory, and organize

40

tournaments. Generally, they are younger individuals, who are working through the career channel of professional golf. They can answer questions, set up lesson schedules, and, as a rule, be most helpful. It is to your benefit to know these people and to be familiar with their jobs.

The pro shop is where you may buy your clubs, balls, gloves, clothing and accessories, as well as other items. Here, you may also meet other playing partners. The pro shop is usually a great location for shop talk and meeting people. Then, after the sport, there is always the "19th Hole," where you can enjoy a cool drink after your round. It's usually located nearby!

On the Course

As you head out toward the first tee, there is often a **starter**. He verifies your starting time, answers questions about the course, and usually accepts the receipt for the green fee.

As you traverse the course, you occasionally encounter an individual in a cart with a "Ranger" sign on it. Some carts may just fly a special flag. **Rangers** have multiple responsibilities. Some of these are:

- To keep play moving at the scheduled pace. This prevents a very slow group or foursome from holding up the play of all the others.
- To check on the progress of various groups as they move through the course. Rangers are usually equipped with phones or radios, which connect with other rangers and the staff in the pro shop.
- To handle emergencies. Should a member of your party become ill while playing or require assistance, contact the closest ranger.

Other staff you may encounter on the course are the **greenkeeper** or course superintendent and his assistants. Greenkeepers are responsible for all course maintenance. They are often college graduates in agronomy or related fields, and they assign their assistants to keep the course mowed, seeded, sprayed, and trimmed. They ensure that the bunkers are raked, flags moved, ball washers cleaned, and tee blocks adjusted on a daily basis.

Among the greenkeeper's problems are weather (that is, too much rain or not enough) as well as those problems presented by the novice player, who may not take responsibility for repairing ball marks on the green, replacing divots, or raking the traps.

Course maintenance is an expensive and time consuming operation. Think of your own lawn and garden at home, and multiply the area to equate the average golf course size of 250 acres. Then factor in the necessary fertilizer, insecticides, seeds, plantings, not to mention sand for bunkers, flags, ball washers, and boundary markers.

The folks out there on tractors work hard in all types of weather. They are also considerate, stopping their engines while you hit your drive or putt and quickly moving out of your line of play. When you are enjoying a round of golf, it's only fair to respect the people whose job it is to make your round pleasant. Be as considerate of them as they are of you!

Another individual who is always a welcome sight on the course is the **refreshment server**. This person drives a beverage cart well-stocked with cold drinks and snacks. He or she is usually able to make change from small bills.

In recent years, former fixtures on the golf course are now seldom seen. Few clubs in America have **caddies**. In other countries, however, such as Mexico, Europe, and Great Britain, caddies are still plentiful. Some courses even feature forecaddies, generally a younger lad, who runs ahead to mark the ball's landing. It is a treat to play in these areas; walking a course with a caddie can be top golf! So if you have the chance to travel abroad, be sure to take your clubs!

Manners and Courtesies

T
he etiquette of golf suggests many little points of courtesy which any player of experience would, from instinctive good breeding, recognize, but there are some little points which, through carelessness, are not always observed, and it would add much to the enjoyment of those playing on the same links, and detract nothing from their own pleasure, if their attention should be called to them. Of course any woman playing in a match whose opponent lost her ball, would, from innate courtesy, try to help her find it, and likewise, no one would think of leaving the tee, having had the honor, before her opponent had played, nor would anyone think, no matter how careless she might be, of moving or speaking while her opponent was preparing or making her shot.
Genevieve Hecker, 1904.

Manners and courtesies rank equally in importance with skills in the game of golf. While volumes could be written on the subject, the written and unwritten rules of golf etiquette can be summed up as follows:

Respect the course and your fellow players!

On the Tee

- The player with the lowest score on the previous hole has the "honor" and should hit the first drive. If the last hole was a tie, then the player with the lowest score on the previous hole hits first.
- Be prepared on the tee and have your club, ball, and tee ready when it is your turn to hit. Stride quickly to the tee box.
- Don't talk when another players is addressing the ball or making a stroke.
- Don't stand too close or crowd another player.
- Be sure other players are out of range before you hit your ball. If you accidentally hit your ball toward other players, yell, "Fore!" to warn them.

On the Fairway

- Allow the player who is farthest from the green to take the first shot. (Two players should not hit at the same time.)
- If you raise a "divot" (plug of grass) when you hit your ball, replace the grass and fill any hole with sand. A divot which has been replaced will quickly grow back; however, one which is not repaired may take six months to return to normal.

In the Bunker

- If your ball lands in a bunker, be sure to rake the sand to cover your footprints and the mark of the ball. This leaves the area clear for the next player.

On the Green

- **Park your cart** to the rear or side of the green. Then you can exit out of the way of approaching players.
- **Don't stand behind the ball** or behind the hole being played. Your presence can be distracting. It is preferable to stand along the line of other players' putts so they can see you while they are putting.
- **Don't step on the line** which extends from another player's ball to the hole. Step over the line or walk around it.
- **Watch your shadow**. Be sure that your shadow does not fall over the line of another player's putt.

- **Mark your ball** with a ball marker before other players putt. If your ball marker is in the line of another player's putt, move the marker over by one or two putter head lengths.

- **Repair the ball mark** (dent your ball makes) on the green. In addition to repairing your own ball mark, it is good practice to repair any other ball mark you may see. A ball mark repair tool can be purchased in the pro shop for a small fee, or a tee can be used for this purpose.

- **Tend the flagstick**. Generally the person whose ball is lying closest to the cup takes responsibility for the flagstick. Flagsticks should be removed when all players have reached the green. A flagstick may be tended when it is difficult to see by the person putting, whether they are on the green or on the short grass adjacent to the green. Hold the flag against the stick so that it does not rattle in the wind. After the player has hit his or her putt, the flagstick should be removed so the ball does not hit it. This is particularly important because a player who is on the green incurs a two-stroke penalty if his or her ball hits the flagstick. There is no penalty for hitting the flagstick if you are putting or hitting from off the green.

- **Take care with the flagstick.** When you remove the flagstick, make sure it does not damage the green. Place it away from the hole so it does not interfere with anyone's putt.

- **Tip:** If you approach the green carrying your putter and an additional club, lay your extra club beside the flagstick. When you replace the flagstick, retrieve your club. Untold numbers of clubs are lost annually by players who drop them beside the green, then walk off to the next tee box, leaving their club behind.

- **Remove your ball** from the cup immediately after completing your putt.

Be Aware of the Time

Golfing is a popular sport, and many courses are crowded. Be conscious of the time and keep your play moving quickly. In general, a foursome should complete nine holes in two hours and 18 holes in four hours. Use your own common sense and avoid unnecessary delays.

Position your cart. If you and your partner drive the ball to opposite sides of the fairway, you can save time by positioning the cart between your ball and the ball of your partner. Then each of you has a short walk to hit your stroke, and you're underway in a minimum of time.

Think ahead. Plan your shots and have your clubs ready when it is your turn to hit the ball. If you have to leave your cart on the cart path and you are not sure which club you are going to hit, carry two or more clubs with you. Always carry an extra ball, ball marker, and tee in your pocket.

Be ready. While the rules of golf say that the player who is farthest from the hole should hit first, many players follow the practice of "ready golf." The player who is ready to hit, hits first.

Save time. Limit the time you spend searching for a lost ball. Generally no more than five minutes should be spent looking for a ball. If necessary, throw down a new ball as close as possible to where your ball was lost, and take the penalty stroke.

Let 'em through. If the hole ahead of you is open and faster players are waiting on the tee, allow them to "play through." Signal by waving your hand, and stand to one side of the fairway so you are not in their line.

Go around. The order of priority on the course are foursomes, threesomes, twosomes, and then a single player. If you are playing alone behind a foursome and the next hole is open, volunteer to go around to the open hole. You are obviously not playing a match, so there is no reason to delay four players while you play through them.

Line up your putt. On the green, line up your putt while others are putting. Just be sure you are not standing in someone else's line or distracting another player. Exit the green promptly so that others can continue their play. Do not record your score while standing on the green; mark the score card on the next tee while other players are hitting.

Save the chit-chat. Golf is a social sport; however, "visiting" should be done in the cart while travelling between strokes and in the clubhouse. Do not delay the game by chit-chatting on the tee, fairway, or green!

Some Other Thoughts

Regardless of your skill level, do not give unsolicited golf lessons to a less able player. Practice areas are the places for lessons, not the golf course.

Statistics report that 50% of golfers have thrown a club at some time in their play. You should be counted among the other 50%. This behavior is childish and can be an embarrassment to other players. If you are having a bad round, and everyone does, keep self-degrading comments to yourself. Your partners are concentrating on their own game and are not particularly concerned with yours.

On most courses, "ball-hawking" (scavenging for lost balls in remote areas of the course) is a no-no. You will see these "hawks" wandering through the brush and peering into ponds, all for the small thrill of finding some unfortunate's beat-up golf ball. They slow up play, and a few get bitten by a snake. The latter outcome is a sure cure for the bad habit. But if they are spared by the snake and persist in the habit, give them one of your own balls, and say, "Partner, let's keep moving."

HOLE	1	2	3	4	5	6	7	8	9	OUT	
BLUE	513	405	416	212	498	399	177	391	402	3413	4(
GOLD	491	358	396	203	484	377	165	367	381	3222	3'
WHITE	471	302	354	189	476	347	125	348	347	2959	3!
PAR	5	4	4	3	5	4	3	4	4	36	
HDCP	15	17	3	5	1	7	13	9	11		1
+/-											
RED	410	279	344	146	401	325	116	283	326	2630	3:
PAR	5	4	4	3	5	4	3	4	4	36	
HDCP	9	13	3	11	1	5	15	17	7		1
DATE:		SCORER:									

Scoring

Words to Know

Par–The number of strokes in which the ideal player will complete the hole. Only the finest golfers will complete the hole in less than "par."

Each hole is assigned a par of either three, four, or five. Par is based on the length of the hole as measured in yards. Pars on the same hole may differ for men and women. In general, for women a par three hole is up to 210 yards, a par four hole is 211-400 yards, and a par five hole is from 401-575 yards.

Handicap–A number assigned to a golfer, which is based on the score he or she normally shoots. The handicap is the difference between a player's average score and the total of par for 18 holes.

Illustrated above is a typical example of a club score card. When starting the game, you need not pay too much attention to your score. Just enjoy being on the course.

Reading the Score Card

Whether or not you will keep score, however, be sure to carry a score card. It often shows the layout of the holes and the position of the hazards, and it always gives the length and the number of strokes which are par for each hole.

Beginning with the top line, you see the hole number. The

48

11	12	13	14	15	16	17	18	IN	TOT	HCP	NET
'04	544	439	158	416	514	389	393	3465	6878		
89	532	379	149	385	493	374	371	3250	6472		
57	498	295	137	371	475	346	348	2977	5936		
3	5	4	3	4	5	4	4	36	72		
10	16	18	4	2	14	8	6				
53	419	287	78	340	422	335	331	2685			
3	5	4	3	4	5	4	4	36	72		
16	6	12	18	4	2	8	10				

ATTEST:

three lines below give you the distance in yards from the specific colored markers to the center of the green. These are the men's tee boxes in descending order of distance. Next is the par line which tells you the designated par for each hole.

The last line before the scoring columns is the hole handicapping for the men's gold and white tees. This number describes the relative difficulty of the hole, with "1" designating the most difficult hole and "18" being the least difficult.

> **Example:** *the handicap square for the fifth hole shows a "1," indicating that it is the most difficult hole on the course. Should Player A have a handicap of 22 and Player B have a handicap of 23, then this is the hole on which Player B would receive an extra uncounted stroke. In a tournament situation, a player with a 23 handicap would receive one free stroke on each of the eighteen holes and an additional stroke on holes labeled with handicaps one through five for a total of 23 free (or uncounted) strokes.*

Scoring

You will note that the typical card provides scoring spaces for four players. Each player's total number of strokes per hole is entered in the appropriate box. The center column is reserved to indicate which two-member team is plus, meaning ahead, or minus, meaning behind, to reflect the standing of the scorer's team.

Example: *the scorer's team wins the first hole. A "+1" would go in the provided square. Should the next hole be tied, then the "+1" would carry forward to that square. In the event the second team wins the third hole, then the teams are tied and a "0" would be entered in this box. In this fashion, a progressive accounting of wins and losses is maintained until completion of the round.*

The next three lines show the distance from the red or ladies' tees followed by the par for that hole. Last is the specific handicap number for that hole. There is also a space provided for the scorer to sign and mark the date and for another player to attest to the accuracy of the score.

At the end of the scoring is a box for the players' total scores; then there is the handicap, which is subtracted from the total score to give each player's net score.

One note of historical interest. Many score cards show a column at the end of the first and second nine labelled, "Out" and "In." These terms refer to the layout of the original Scottish "links" style courses, in which the first nine holes were laid out away from the starting point along the shoreline, and the second nine returned in.

Reminders
- Check your score for errors.
- Be sure the card is signed by the scorer and attested.
- Turn your card in as requested to maintain a current and accurate handicap.

Handicapping

Golf is unique. Unlike tennis, it is a game a solo player can thoroughly enjoy. Golf is also a game that one can comfortably play with just about anyone else. This is made possible by a system known as "handicapping," which makes it possible for any golfer to play with another golfer regardless of their degree of skill.

Of course, first you have to get a handicap. Let's take the example of Ann Jones, a beginner at the game. Ann has had four or five lessons from the pro at the course where her husband plays. She has played a few rounds with lady friends, who suggest she obtain a handicap to make the game more interesting and to make foursome matches possible.

To establish her handicap, Ann will turn in her score cards at the pro shop or enter her scores into the computer, if the course is so equipped. A minimum of five scores must be entered before a handicap can be established, and it will be based on the lowest score. Of course, the more scores that are entered, the more accurate the handicap will be. After 20 scores have been entered, the ten lowest scores will be used to establish a handicap. In our example, let's say Ann's average is 40 strokes above the par for the course, which is 72 strokes.

Ann now has a handicap of 40. She would like to play with her best friend, who has been playing a bit longer, and is naturally a better golfer. Her friend has a handicap of 25. Therefore, to make their golf match fair and fun, Ann is entitled to reduce her score by 15 strokes, the difference between her handicap and that of her friend.

Now, we look at the score card. In the column that gives the handicap for each hole that has a number of 15 or less, Ann will receive one free stroke. Should she score an eight on any one of these holes, for competitive purposes, her score would be noted as a seven. In essence, the handicap equalizes the playing ability among opponents, making all golfers as evenly matched as possible on the course.

Should Ann want to play on another course which is more or less difficult than her own, her handicap can be adapted to that course through the use of the handicap index. The handicap index is a calculation of the degree of difficulty of a golf course. It is a number given to you by your home course, and it allows you to travel from course to course and still have the advantage of playing with an appropriate handicap. To determine your handicap on an unfamiliar course, consult the Handicap Table posted in the pro shop or ask the pro or assistant pro for assistance.

The Games People Play

Hey! There is a lot of fun to be had here. When your playing chums drop names like "Nassau" or "Skins," you can look knowledgeable and say, "I prefer a 50 cent Nassau" or whatever!

Match vs. Medal

There are two basic forms of competition: match or medal (also called stroke) play. Match play is hole score against hole score. Whoever has the lowest score wins the hole. The total number of holes won out of the 18 determines the winner.

In medal (or stroke) play, the winner is the one with the lowest number of strokes for the 18 holes. Simple enough!

Scramble

Now, here is a fun game, especially for beginners, since you are not committed to your bad shots. In a scramble, all four players on your team hit their drives. Then the best drive is selected by the captain, who is generally the low handicap player. Each player drops a ball at that spot and shoots. This process is repeated until the ball is holed. Scores can be surprisingly low since you are only hitting the very best ball from four players. But be careful! Even four players can miss a four-foot putt, one after the other.

Best Ball

This is simple and played the world over. It's two against two in a foursome. Let's say that on the first hole, you shoot a six, and your partner pars with a four. Your two opponents each score a five. You win the hole, because your partner has the low ball with a four.

This format can be varied such as low ball, low total. In the example above, you would receive one point for the low ball and no points for low total because you and your opponents tied at ten apiece. Had you scored a five instead of a six, then your total of nine would have beaten their ten, winning you an additional half point. At the end of 18 holes, the points are totalled, and the winners receive so much a point. This is provided you can collect your winnings! Regardless, it is customary for the winners to buy the first round at the "19th Hole."

Nassau

This can be played for any amount of money. For this example, we will use $1. There is a dollar bet on the first nine holes. The team or individual who wins the most holes in that nine wins the dollar. The procedure is duplicated on the second nine holes for the next dollar. The winner of the most holes out of the total 18 wins the third dollar. Thus, in our example, you could win or loose $3 at the most.

Six-Six-Six

Whatever the betting game in this format, you change partners every six holes. In this fashion, you have had each of the other three players as a partner for one six-hole play during an 18-hole round.

Pinehurst

Here, you and your partner each drive from the tee. If your partner's is the best shot, then you would hit his ball and he would hit next, alternating shots unto the cup.

Trash Bets

There are many of these and they can be played for any amount. The following are but a few, usually 50 cents a bet.

Greenies - Winner is the ball hit from the tee to the green and closest to the hole on a par three.

Sandie - Any player wins a "Sandie" by coming from a green-side bunker in one shot and sinking the first putt.

Birdies - Fifty cents to any player who birdies a hole.

Bingle - Bangle - Bongle

This is often played when you have only three players. A point (you set the value) is awarded for the first player on the green, a point for the player nearest the hole, and the last point for the first player into the cup.

Skins

A point is awarded to the low ball for each hole. If the low ball is a tie, there is no winner. "Two tie, all tie" as the expression goes. You may play this with carry-overs, meaning the next hole is doubled after a tie. Be careful, this can mount up.

These are a few of the most popular games. There are many more; however, a familiarity with the games described above is sufficient for now.

The Golf Tournament

S ooner or later, you are likely to find yourself involved in a golf tournament as a player, volunteer helper, or even chairman for the event. Golf tournaments are a popular means of raising funds for charitable organizations; they may also be a part of the recreational program for a corporate outing.

You don't have to be an experienced golfer to participate in the tournament planning process. Many excellent tournament organizers have never swung a golf club, but produce excellent results for their employers or service groups by becoming familiar with the principles of sound tournament planning. So, if you are assigned to a tournament planning committee, good organizational skills and some familiarity with the game of golf will be helpful.

Plan Ahead

You can't begin the planning process too early. There's a lot to do, and advance planning will ease the way. A typical planning committee will include a tournament director, with other members assigned to invite players, publicize the event, contact donors and hole sponsors, gather prizes, and coordinate volunteers.

Set your Goals

Make sure that everyone is in agreement about what you hope to accomplish through your tournament. Some typical goals are (1) to raise funds for a specific purpose; (2) to gain exposure and recognition for your organization; (3) to allow golfers the opportunity to compete with others; or (4) to provide members of your organization with an enjoyable recreational experience. The more specific you can be about your goals, the easier the planning process will become.

Identify your Tournament Sponsors

Depending on the goals you have set for your tournament, you may want to identify some major sponsors who can help to defray the costs of the event. Possible donors include vendors who do business with your organization and those who are known personally by members of your committee. You may want to decide in advance what level of contribution to request. Donors may "sponsor" a hole; contribute funds to purchase special prizes or "extras," such as shirts, hats, towels, golf balls; or donate merchandise, a dinner for two, or round of golf at an area course.

Some sponsoring organizations are able to contribute a major prize, such as a car or a trip to Europe. Typically, these prizes are only awarded if a player makes a hole-in-one on a par-three hole. All major sponsors should receive special recognition in all tournament publicity.

Hole Sponsors

If the purpose of your tournament is to raise funds, you will want to try to attract as many "hole sponsors" as you can. A hole sponsor is an individual or corporate donor who contributes a specified amount in exchange for the display of his own or his company's name on a sign, generally placed around the tee area of a golf hole. Hole sponsorships can cost from $100 to $1,000, depending on what the market will bear, and may include the registration fee for one or more golfers. You are not limited to 18 hole sponsors; it is acceptable to display more than one hole sponsor sign on a hole. In soliciting hole sponsors, there is no substitute for a personal contact; a form letter to a prospective donor will rarely be sufficient.

Select a Date and Time

Golf tournaments can be held on any day of the week; however, weekends will generally attract the largest number of golfers. Many women's tournaments can be scheduled during the week if the players are not employed full-time. Some private clubs will only hold a tournament on days when they are "closed" so that their members' play times are not restricted. Mondays are the most popular day for tournaments at private clubs.

If your tournament is a fund raiser, try to find a day when it will not be in conflict with another or follow too closely after another organization's event.

It is advisable to schedule your tournament at a time when the weather will be the most agreeable. In hot climates, a morning tee-time is preferable. Some tournaments will arrange staggered tee-times, while others offer a "shot-gun" start with all play beginning at the same time on different holes.

Meals can be scheduled before, after, and even during play. If before play, the meal should be light and nutritious. Some tournaments provide a sack lunch to be eaten during play. A meal following play is usually combined with an awards ceremony.

Choose a Place

Tournaments can be held at private clubs or public courses. You will want to talk to the golf professionals at several courses before making a final decision. Take into consideration what dates they are able to offer you and what is included in the package. The course will charge you a set fee for each golfer. Some courses will handle the registration of golfers for you, while others expect your group to handle the paperwork. You will also want to get quotes from the course or club's catering/ banquet service for refreshments or a meal before or after play.

Determine the Tournament Format

There are a number of different tournament formats from which to choose. The golf professional at your course or club will be happy to advise you as to which one would be most suitable.

A scramble format allows play to move along quickly since each team of four players hits from the best shot from among the team.

A best-ball format requires all players to play out their own balls; however, only the lowest score on each hole is counted.

For two-person teams, a two-ball format allocates only one ball per team. Partners alternate playing shots; one member drives from the even-numbered tees, and the other from the odd-numbered tees.

Some formats are particularly popular for couples. In a Mixed Foursome or Pinehurst, partners alternate driving from each tee and then play alternate shots until the ball is holed out. One modification of this format allows both partners to drive from each tee and then select which ball to play. In a third option, both partners drive and then hit a second shot with the other's ball. After the second shot, the team selects which ball to play and alternates shots until the hole is completed.

You will also want to decide if you will allow players to purchase one or more "Mulligans" (free second shots) and whether the Mulligan may be used only from the tee or anywhere on the hole.

Many tournaments also include mini-contests for "closest to the pin" on par three holes; longest drives, straightest drives, and monster putts.

Publicize your Tournament

Once you have selected a date, time, location, and format, you are ready to begin to publicize the tournament. A theme or special tournament logo can help attract attention for your event. Remember your goals and select a theme or visual that is in keeping with the spirit of your tournament.

It is a good idea to develop a small poster, which can be displayed on golf course bulletin boards and in golf shop windows. You will also want to design a flier/registration form, which can be mailed directly to prospective golfers.

A press release about your tournament should be sent to the sports or golf editor of your local newspapers. Radio and television stations as well as cable television companies will accept public service announcements publicizing your tournament. In some communities, a golfing newspaper carries a monthly schedule of tournaments. Be sure to include information on how to register.

Players

Lists of prospective players can often be obtained from area courses or clubs, although some private clubs will not release their membership list to non-members. In such cases, ask the club to display your poster and registration forms and include mention of your tournament in their monthly newsletter. Registration forms and posters should also be distributed to area golf outlets. It is a good idea to set a deadline for registration that is three or four days in advance of the tournament date. While you may accept walk-ins on the day of the tournament, it is helpful to know in advance how many players to expect.

Handouts and Prizes

It is customary to distribute handouts or "goody bags" to all players. These may include a golf towel, hat, shirt, snack item, gift certificate, raffle tickets, and other inexpensive gift items.

Everyone likes to win, and a fun tournament makes everyone a winner. A good supply of prizes will please your players and bring them back year after year. Golfers love to win rounds of golf at other courses or resorts, and golf gadgets and balls are always well received. Meals for two at local restaurants are among other popular giveaways.

Volunteers

On the day of the tournament, you will need plenty of help. Volunteers may be asked to register golfers, position hole sponsor signs, hand out "goody bags," take photographs, sell Mulligans and raffle tickets, distribute beverages or snacks, and monitor such mini-contests as the monster putt and hole-in-one attempts.

After the Tournament

You can't say enough "Thank yous." Sponsors should receive a special expression of appreciation by letter or in person. It is a good idea to thank your players as well. One popular followup is a listing of the tournament results and a picture of each four-some for your participants. If your tournament was a fund-raiser, be sure to let players and sponsors know how the moneys were spent. Finally, get together with your committee, critique the event, and make some notes for next year's tournament.

Fun Tournament Formats

Some other popular tournament ideas are described below. Ask your club professional for advise as to what format would be appropriate for your group.

No Alibi Tournament—In this format, each player is allowed to replay a number of shots which is equal to three quarters of his or her handicap. The replayed ball must be played out, even if it is worse than the first ball struck.

Par Battle—In this format, players are informed that on 10 holes, they will receive five extra points for scoring par or better. On three holes, players can earn 10 extra points for scoring par or better. On three other holes, players who do not score par or better will be penalized five points. On the remaining two holes, the penalty will be 10 points for failing to score par or better. The winner or winning team accumulates the most points at the end of the round.

String Tournament—Instead of a handicap, each player or team is given a string measured out to a distance equal to one foot for each handicap stroke. During the round, players may advance the ball to a better position by measuring off the distance the ball was moved with the string and cutting off the length used. The ball may be moved to improve a difficult lie or out of a hazard. On the green, the ball may even be advanced into the cup! When the string is used up, however, the player may no longer move the ball.

Throw-Out Tournament—At the conclusion of the round, each player is allowed to eliminate his three worst holes from his final score. Handicaps are usually adjusted accordingly.

"Weather" or Not

Golf can be played in all kinds of weather — hot or cold, rain or shine. Certain precautions should be taken, however, and the right equipment is a must!

Rain

Playing in a light rain is fine. There is a Scottish saying, "If it ain't coming sideways, it ain't raining." To make playing in the rain more enjoyable, make sure your equipment includes the following:

- **Gloves** — At least three or four pairs. Your hands and club grips must be kept dry. For the latter, a bag hood is essential. It goes without saying that you need to carry an umbrella — a large one.
- **Shoes** — waterproof are the best, but water-repellent is OK.
- **Suits** — waterproof rain suits are now made that fold into very small pouches and are easily carried in a golf bag. Buy a good one, or you will waste your money.
- **Towels** — carry two or three small ones for drying grips, hands, etc.

Cold

The solution to cold weather is to dress warmly, but loosely. One good cold-weather outfit is thermal underwear, a turtleneck, a vest or sweater, and a lightweight windbreaker. Cotton or wool slacks are fine, and some players like warmup suits.

Two pairs of socks beat one, and calf-length is best. For your head, a good old Navy watch cap is fine — the kind that you can roll down over your ears. You can also carry ear muffs, or try a hat with flaps that cover your ears.

Many players now carry the chemical handwarmers, and some own cart covers, which offer good insulation from the chill when you are driving from shot to shot. Be sure to drive carefully; the visibility through a cart cover is not the best.

In summation, stay warm, but do not let your clothing restrict your movements. Remember, light layering is much better than loading yourself down with heavy, bulky clothing.

Heat

Here again, it's a good idea carrying a towel or two. Your hands can become just as moist from the heat as from the rain. Spare gloves are also helpful. Light, loose clothing is a must. How Gary Player toured the southern states in summer while wearing all black is a mystery!

Use sunscreen and carry bug repellent. At the water fountains, a cold wet towel applied to the back of the neck is most helpful. Always drink plenty of water. If water is not readily available, carry a thermos or a bottle of frozen water with you. Placed in an insulated container, such as those used for beer, it will stay cold for a very long period of time. A good, light-colored, wide-brim head cover is strongly recommended.

Don't "pig out" at the turn. A light energy snack is best, and, again, drink lots and lots of water. A dash of lemon may be added for flavor.

Lightning

Here we go — and you may have heard it before: the golf course is not where you want to be in a storm. First, check the weather reports before leaving for the course. Sheet lightning apparently at a distance may appear harmless; however, golfers have been struck from almost cloudless skies.

The safest place in a lightning storm is in a large building, not a small shack on the course. Golf carts do not offer protection. If it is not possible to return to the clubhouse, the best bet is to seek out low-lying ground with small trees.

There are some players who always want to get in just one more hole. That's when you say, "Ladies, I am heading for the barn!," and mean it. Beaches and golf courses are traditionally bad news when it comes to lightning. Please remember — don't chance it — use common sense.

The Physical

Women have certain physical advantages over men in any athletic activity. Their principle advantage is flexibility; obviously, their main disadvantage is strength.

Many small, talented ladies can power a golf ball farther than the average male. Proof of this fact is readily available if you watch an LPGA tournament on TV. Much of the field is slim and trim; however, they are all in shape. They have to be in order the play the game the way they do.

The game of golf does require a certain amount of agility and strength. You presently may be doing aerobics, jogging, swimming, or hiking in your own personal fitness program. And, that is great. Listed below are a few pointers specifically designed to help you get in shape or stay shape for golf.

Stretches for Flexibility

Described below are some simple stretching exercises adapted from an exercise program designed for women golfers. They can be done at home on the family room floor, and they not only benefit your golf game, but will also keep you in shape for your everyday activities.

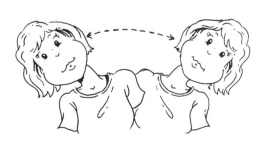

1. Neck Stretch.
Sit in a chair and hold onto the base of the seat with your right hand; lean left and stretch your left ear towards your left shoulder. Repeat on the alternate side.

2. Calf Stretch

Stand facing a wall with your feet shoulder width apart. Place your hands against the wall at shoulder height, and place your left foot back. Bend your right knee as much as possible while keeping your left knee straight and both heels flat on the floor. Feel the stretch in the calf muscle. Alternate on opposite side.

3. Trunk Rotation Stretch

Sit on the floor and cross your left leg over your extended right leg. Place your left hand on the floor behind you, and rotate your upper body left, placing your right hand against the outside of your left thigh. Using your right hand, pull the thigh further into the stretch. Alternate on opposite side.

4. Hamstring Stretch

Sit on the floor with legs extended and spread in front of you. Starting on the right side, lean forward over your right knee, placing your hands on your right ankle. Lean into the stretch and hold for a count of 10. Repeat over the left leg and then straight forward between your legs.

5. Knee to Shoulder Stretch

Lie on your back with both legs straight. Grab your left knee and pull it toward your right shoulder. Repeat on alternate side.

Exercises for Building Strength

Described below are some exercises designed to build strength and endurance in the muscle groups which are particularly important for your golf game. Try them three times a week, with at least one day of rest in-between. Start with just a few repetitions, and gradually work towards increasing the number of repetitions of each exercise.

1. Counter Top Pushups

Place your hands on a waist-high counter top a little wider than shoulder-width apart. Back away from the counter until your arms are at a 90 degree angle from your body. Slowly lower yourself toward the counter until your chest touches the edge. Push back to the starting position, keeping your body straight and your weight on the balls of your feet. Repeat twice, rest, and repeat in sets of three up to ten sets.

2. Shoulder Extension

Rest one hand on a counter top and hold a weight with the other. With arm extended, pull the weight back until the arm is parallel with the floor. Hold for one count and then lower the arm. Repeat on the opposite side.

3. Shoulder External Rotation

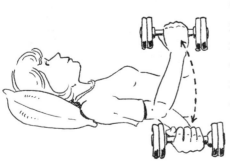

Lie on your side with your head supported with one hand, while the other arm lies close to your ribs. Raise the weight until it is pointed upward, then lower to the starting position. Repeat several times on one side and then reverse.

4. Shoulder Internal Rotation

Lie on your back. With right arm held against your ribs and your elbow extended at 90 degrees from your body, raise the weight from the floor until it points to the ceiling. Lower back to the starting point. Repeat on the alternate side.

5. Chair Squats

Stand behind one chair and in front of another.

Holding onto the back of the chair in front of you, slowly lower yourself toward the seat of the other chair. Hold the squat position just over the chair seat, then raise yourself to an upright position. Repeat.

6. Rapid Finger Flexion

Hold your arms outstretched and open and close your fingers as fast as you can.

Make sure you spread your hand as wide as you can, and close it firmly.

Diet

Here are just a few "no's" and some "yes's," which will make your game more enjoyable.

"Yes's"

- Drink plenty of water. You can carry it with you, or take advantage of the many drinking fountains located on the course.
- Carry a snack with you on the course such as an energy bar, fruit, or crackers.
- If a meal such as breakfast or lunch precedes a round of golf, try to make it an energy meal, rich with carbohydrates such as pasta or cereal.

"No's"

- Caffeine can give you the "yipps." Stay away from it preceding and during a round.
- If you're a bit hungry after playing nine holes, a light snack at the turn is fine. Leave the heavy hamburgers, chili dogs,

and triple-decker sandwiches until after the round.

- In spite of what you may see offered on the beverage wagon, alcohol is a "no." Aside from inhibiting your play, rest stop facilities for ladies on the course are few and far between. Why disrupt the play of your partners while you spring across fairways looking for the nearest comfort station?

Lesson Time

There are any number of ways to get started in golf, and many avenues of instruction available to you. Sometimes a family member or friend doubles as golf coach. Tread carefully here. While occasionally you can pick up valuable pointers from a friendly observer, there is no substitute for professional instruction, particularly for a beginner.

There are also countless instructional books, written or ghost-written by famous professionals. Some professionals have also produced their own instructional videos. These can help to explain and illustrate the fundamentals of the game.

Sooner or later, however, almost everyone takes a formal lesson from a golf professional.

Selecting an Instructor

The selection of your golf teacher is a very important decision. Instructors may be contacted through clubs, as well as semi-private and public courses or driving ranges. You can also ask your golfing friends for recommendations. The selection of the right instructor for you, however, is a very personal choice.

It is very important that you feel comfortable with your instructor. When you are taking up a new sport, it is natural to feel awkward and ill at ease. You need to feel that your instructor is on your side and that he or she speaks your language. You will have many questions you will want to ask! Don't be embarrassed; you won't be the first to have asked them.

Who is a Golf Professional?

Members of the Professional Golf Association or PGA are considered to be the most highly qualified instructors. These individuals are high school graduates who have completed a three-year apprenticeship under a Class A PGA professional. They must also have taken a requisite number of business school and college courses as well as passed a playing test and an oral examination. An instructor who has achieved the status of a PGA master professional has acquired over 20 years experience in the field and has written a thesis.

An increasing number of professional golf instructors are graduates of college or university programs in professional golf management. Another new trend in the field of professional golf is the increasing number of women PGA professionals!

How to Schedule a Lesson

When you call to schedule a lesson, let your instructor know your level of playing ability. If you are a brand new golfer, let him know that this will be your first experience with the game. If you have been playing for a while and have identified a specific problem with your game, let him know that too. Many players schedule periodic lessons as a preventive measure, almost like making regular visits to the doctor for medical check-ups. The most common reason given for seeking professional help is to improve distance and accuracy.

Ask your instructor the length of time the lesson will last. Typical lessons range from 30 minutes to one hour. Also ask about the charge and preferred method of payment, cash, check, etc. You may also want to inquire if the instructor offers a discount for a series of lessons.

Be sure to specify where you will meet your instructor. You may be asked to go directly to the driving range or to meet in the Pro Shop.

Group Lessons

Many beginners are introduced to the game through a group lesson or golf clinic. Your club or public course may offer a series of three to six lessons for new golfers. In these classes, the instructor will give general instruction to the group, and, if time permits, offer specific pointers to individual players.

One distinct advantage of the group lesson is that you are introduced to some other new players with whom you can practice. Group lessons are also generally less expensive.

What to Wear and What to Bring

Necessary golf equipment includes the following: golf shoes, a glove, clubs, balls, tees, and a hat or visor. Beginners often ask if they need to wear golf shoes. Most instructors say golf shoes are not required, but the shoes they wear for the lesson should offer good support.

A glove is not absolutely necessary for the first lesson, but it allows you to get a firm grip on the club and protects your hand. Remember, right handers wear the golf glove on their left hand and vice versa. Gloves cost between $7 and $15, and can be purchased anywhere golf equipment is sold.

If you do not have your own clubs, be sure to ask if clubs are available for rent or if the necessary club(s) can be borrowed for the duration of the lesson. Balls and tees are generally provided by the instructor.

When to Arrive

You should always plan on arriving earlier than the scheduled beginning time of the lesson. If it is your first lesson, this will allow you to get your equipment together and complete any necessary paperwork. On subsequent lessons, arrive early and be sure to warm up. The golf swing places considerable strain on the back muscles, so you should work up to the full swing gradually. The warm-up will also help you to find a rhythm for your swing. When the pro arrives, you will be ready to go!

What to Expect

During your first lesson, you will learn how to grip the club, how to stand, and how to align the club head with the ball. Many instructors start with the short game of putting and chipping and/or some mid-length iron shots. Gradually you will work up to hitting the woods and the driver.

After your first lesson, you will have learned how to hit a golf ball, even if you can't hit it very far. Be sure to find out from your instructor what you should practice and if there is an area of the course which is suitable for that purpose. Many courses have chipping areas as well as driving ranges and practice putting greens. Ask also about recommended exercises and a warm-up routine.

How to Pay for the Lesson

Charges for instruction will vary depending on the area in which you live and the level of expertise of your instructor. As of this writing, the going rate for an individual golf lesson ranges from $20 to $40.

You can pay your instructor either before or after the lesson. Many instructors recommend that you pay before the lesson begins. This leaves time at the end of the lesson to review the session and discuss practice tips. Often instructors are pressed for time at the conclusion of the lesson because they have another appointment scheduled.

Before the Next Lesson - Practice!

Many beginners will sprint for the first tee after their first lesson. Once on the course, you must play with the "swing you brung." This is not the place to learn. Practice, but only in designated areas. There will be plenty of time to play the course when you have progressed to a comfortable playing level.

A point to remember, and it can't be said often enough: the short game of chipping, pitching, and putting accounts for half of your golf strokes. Dedicate at least half of your practice time to these critical score-savers. Plan on having several practice sessions before your next lesson.

Scheduling the Second or Third Lesson

After you have had one or two lessons from your instructor you should know if the chemistry is right between you. The more comfortable you feel with your instructor, the more quickly you will progress. Don't hesitate to make a change if you find someone with whom you are more compatible.

Have Fun!

If this is beginning to sound too much like work, don't worry. It's fun! There are always new techniques to learn and new equipment to try. Players at every level benefit from instruction and enjoy the improvements they make in their game. You will too!

Golf Schools

Pick up any golf magazine, and you will find advertised a number of "golf schools." These sessions typically last from four to six days and offer intensive group instruction. Charges for golf schools generally include meals and lodging at attractive golf resorts. Golf schools can be expensive, but they make a nice vacation and offer opportunities to meet other golfers. A listing of golf schools can be obtained from the National Golf Foundation (407) 744-6006, FAX (407) 744-9085.

How To Link Think

Your mental approach to the game of golf is just as vital a contribution to your playing ability as any degree of physical skill you may develop. Golf is not a typical reaction sport, in which your opponent takes action and you respond.

Your strategy and thoughts are meshed in a more lengthy time frame, from stroke to stroke and from hole to hole. Thus, it follows that immediately following a mis-hit shot or a ball landing in the water or out-of-bounds, one side of your brain is going to give you a fit. For example, you are likely to tell yourself: "That was just stupid!" "I knew I should have used a five iron instead of a six!" "I am playing like an idiot, like I never before had a club in my hand!"

These thoughts are the fastest track to another bad shot. Instead of scolding yourself for your mistakes, let's "accentuate the positive," as the old song goes. Tell yourself instead: "Aw heck! (or whatever). In any round, I am going to hit some very bad shots, some not so bad, and some great ones. If all my shots were great, I'd be on the tour, rather than toting a 22 handicap here at Sand and Swamp County Club!"

Even the great Sam Snead has bad shots in a round. *When you have 'em, you forget 'em.* Remember only the good swings.

Don't hover. It won't hatch!

Do: Walk up to your ball. Take your alignment and picture in your mind only a beautiful flight of the ball with a crisp bounce just where you want it to land. THEN SWING.

Don't: "Gee, I put one in the water here yesterday." "Maybe this isn't the right club." "I've got to par this hole to have any kind of score." "Am I swinging too hard or is my backswing too fast." These are trash thoughts. First they trash your mind, then they trash your swing, next they trash your game!

Always picture the ball going in the hole from any length putt, from any chip shot, from any green-side bunker.

When putting, think only of the best putts you have sunk. Thus you know what you are capable of doing. Throw out the trash thoughts, e.g. "Will it go left?" "I can't leave it short." "But I don't want to hit it too hard either."

Putting is more than fifty percent mental. With proper professional instruction, anyone can learn to putt a ball along a reasonably straight line into a hole over four inches wide. The reason we don't do it is because all the doubts and negatives are piling up in our minds, crowding out the only two things needed.

Which Are: I see the line. With a practice swing, I know the force. Now hit the ball. Don't stand there hovering until you get the tremors. It won't hatch, so hit it!

In Sum

Some key concepts in forming a helpful mental attitude toward golf are as these: confidence, concentration, and relaxation.

Confidence. The champions seem to glow with it, and it helps to make them what they are. But, it's no less important for the amateur. While confidence may not guarantee that every shot will be your best, without question, a lack of it will undermine your best efforts. Think your best, and more often than not, you'll end up doing it.

Concentration. One of the most fascinating aspects of the game is that from day to day, and from shot to shot, it's never the same. Changes in weather and wind direction, not to mention changes in your position on the course, make each shot different. To do your best, you must focus not only on the mechanics of your swing but also take in the variables of your surroundings.

Relaxation. By this is meant the ability to remove tension from your body and mind. As you progress in the techniques of hitting a golf ball, you will learn which muscles to tense and to what degree. What you want to avoid is unnecessary tension, either physical or mental, because it will destroy your game. So, clear your mind, relax your body, and enjoy the game.

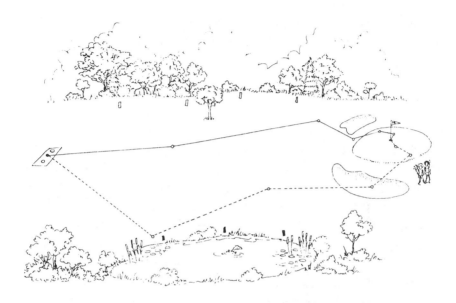

Let's Play 14

Now, let's visit to a sample hole on a typical course. With a ladies handicap rating of six, the fourteenth hole at Swampside Country Club is a 360-yard straight par four (see illustration). There is an out-of-bounds area on the left side of the fairway, which abuts a highway. This area is indicated by the white stakes. For some distance down the right side of the fairway is a lateral water hazard, marked by red stakes.

The distance markers from the center of the green are small evergreens at 150 and 100 yards out. There are two bunkers guarding the green, and the flagstick (pin) is located in the center of the green. This is indicated by a white flag. (A red flag would indicate that the pin was placed at the front of the green, blue to the rear. Some courses use a round globe attached to the pin that is slid upward as the flag is moved to the rear.)

Ann Jones has played for almost two years, and her handicap

is down to a very respectable 27. She still must guard against a tendency to slice her drives and fairway woods off to the right. On the plus side, she is a very good putter and chipper, having put in almost half of her practice time on this phase of the game. It is here around the green that women and men and physically equal.

Player (A) Ann's tee shot (dotted line) is a slice 120 yards down the fairway. Her opponent, Player (B), an 18-handicap, drives 160 yards down the middle (straight line).

Ann's second shot is better: a three-wood that puts her 100 yards short of the green. Ann's third shot is unfortunate — a mis-hit six-iron that rolls into the right bunker. Out of the bunker, she now lies four on the rear portion of the green.

Her opponent is short with her wedge shot, and chips to within seven feet of the pin. Ann is down in two putts for a hole score of six. Her opponent misses the seven-footer, makes the tap-in putt, and also takes six strokes.

Nonetheless, Ann wins the hole. The fourteenth hole at Swampside is the six handicap hole. Thus Ann has a free stroke that is not counted, giving her a net of five on the hole.

The Ninety Degree Rule

One final note about our hypothetical Swampside course. This is a course that enforces a 90 degree rule, one that you will find in effect on a number of courses. It simply means that you do not take your cart straight down the fairway from shot to shot.

For example, you have hit your tee shot 150 yards down the center of the fairway. The golf cart is then driven down the cart path to a position off the fairway, but opposite to your ball. Here, you turn 90 degrees and drive directly to your ball. After you shoot, you return on the same route to the cart path.

Partners

One of the many distinct benefits of the game of golf is the people you will meet and the new friends you will make as you play it. The sport offers countless opportunities for such contacts.

Most clubs and courses plan specific weekly playing times for women such as "Ladies' Day." Ladies' associations organize "Nine Hole" and "Eighteen Hole" groups. These groups offer competitive play for women, which is open to players of all levels. Inter-club matches and ladies' invitational tournaments also offer opportunities to meet new players. Some clubs also sponsor outings to out-of-town courses.

As mentioned before, beginners' clinics may be offered specifically for women, some of which are designed to accommodate a working woman's schedule. The "Executive Women's" group, which plays on weekends, is an increasingly popular feature at many courses.

Another enjoyable way to become involved in the game is through events designed for mixed foursomes. These events include couples' "Hilly Dilly" tournaments and short games in the late afternoon in a variety of formats, many of which conclude with social events. They accommodate players of all levels, and beginners often feel very comfortable playing in them. No, you don't have to be married to a golfer in order to participate! The organizer in the pro shop will pair you up with someone who is looking for a partner.

Increasingly women are taking golf clubs with them when they travel — even when travelling alone and on business. Often time is set aside for recreation during a business conference, and golf can be a great way to pass the time. Again, don't worry about having a partner in tow. The pro shop will pair you with a partner or a threesome who are looking for a fourth. Call ahead if you can, and give the pro or assistant pro information about your handicap at your home course.

A Personal Note

Depending on your level of interest in the game, you may find that you are more compatible with some players than you are with others. This is perfectly natural. You don't enjoy having lunch with everyone listed in your address book. Nor will you enjoy a four-hour round of golf with everyone you know or chance to meet.

What is vitally important, however, is that you observe the long established rules of courtesy with everyone you encounter. Nothing is more destructive to club or course morale than "catty" or "behind-the-back" criticism of another player. If you encounter it in the ladies' locker room, stay clear. It does you no credit to engage in such conversations, and your non-participation may discourage it.

When Your Work is Play

Mix golf and a professional career? It's a natural! While a woman who is working 40+ hours a week has less time for golf than one who is retired or employed part-time, there are many advantages to combining golf with a career.

Take a Break!

The first and most obvious is that golf is a wonderful way to relax and take your mind off the pressures of a job. Golf is totally absorbing. You can't be lining up a putt while thinking about tomorrow's staff meeting. Golf is relaxing, restoring, and generally rehabilitating. In addition, it's played in the great outdoors, which makes it all the more enjoyable.

Contacts! Contacts! Contacts!

Golf is first and foremost a social sport and a great way to meet people. To use a contemporary buzzword, it affords wonderful opportunities for "networking," and someone you meet through your golf club or course may serve to be a useful contact on your job.

We might point out here that these opportunities are relatively new for women. In the early days of the sport, most clubs did not admit women onto the golf course; the links were a domain reserved for males only! Ladies will still find hangovers of this out-dated tradition in certain conservative clubs, such as Burning Tree outside Washington D.C., and on the sacred ground of many clubs' Men's Grills.

Today, however, almost all clubs are open to ladies, although some still restrict certain tee times for men only. Many clubs are working hard to attract women golfers, and schedule group lessons, clinics and weekend tournaments specifically for professional women. There may also be a chapter of the Executive Women's Golf League or comparable organization in your community. Call (407) 471-1477 for information on EWGL.

"Getting to Know You!"

More than one person has said that you can find out more about an individual in a single round of golf than you can in a dozen lunches or business meetings. During four hours on the course, you have a unique opportunity to observe a person's temperament and personality. Is your playing partner aggressive? Competitive? Conservative? Creative? Methodical? What you learn about your colleagues on the golf course may give you some useful insights as to how they will function in the Board Room or during a sales call.

Golf on the Road

If your job calls for travel, pack your clubs. Part of the fun of golf is trying out new courses, and nine holes in the late afternoon or early morning gives you something to look forward to on a business trip. Of course, many business conferences and conventions are held at golf resorts and times for golf are worked into the schedule of events.

"Swinging" a Deal?

You will hear some people say that they conduct business on the golf course. Perhaps, but exercise caution here. If your playing partners are serious about golf, they will not want to be negotiating a sale while extricating a ball from a bunker. And, if they're serious about business, they may feel it is more appropriately conducted in conventional settings.

While a matter of business may be brought up casually on the course, deals you can take to the bank are more typically confirmed over a ham and rye in the clubhouse. Of course there are exceptions to this rule, but use discretion and let your partner be the one to introduce a business or work-related topic. Remember golf is for fun, for relaxation, and for friendship.

Kids on the Course

While you're getting your own game off the ground, you don't have to leave the kids at home. Golf is a great family game, and kids will benefit from an early start.

A Healthy Pursuit

Golf is a great sport for young people. First of all, it's safe. Kids rarely get hurt playing golf; it's far less risky that many contact sports. It's not overly competitive; the golfer's number one adversary is himself as he works to improve his score. Finally, golf rewards those who exercise discipline, control, and good judgement — all positive and enviable character traits.

Team up for Lessons

Most clubs and public courses offer group classes and clinics for junior golfers. These sessions may be offered after school, but are most often scheduled during the summer months, so make your inquiries about programs during the spring. The responsibility of teaching youngsters is often assigned to one of the assistant pros, who relates well to children. As with most new ventures, it's a good idea to have your child bring a friend. Then he will have a golfing buddy with whom to practice.

Equipment

Today there are a number of junior clubs and starter sets on the market specifically designed for children. Of course, your child can take his first swings with mom or dad's clubs or even with a toy set.

For the best and most successful results, however, make sure the club is light enough so that your child can swing it easily. The grip should be small enough for a child's fingers to hold, and the shaft should be flexible. Woods should have plenty of loft so that your child can get the ball off the ground.

It is not necessary to have a full set of clubs — a putter, a nine iron, a seven or five wood constitute a good beginner's set. If your child continues to be interested in the game, add a seven or five iron. Stash the clubs in a lightweight, nylon golf bag that's easy to carry, and your child is ready to head for the links.

Golf Camps

Another option for a beginning junior golfer is a junior golf camp. A variety of summer camp options are offered for youngsters aged 10 to 18 years and for beginning, intermediate, and advanced playing levels. Most camps involve a mixture of golf instruction and other recreational activities. Sessions fill up early, so for best selection, make your plans in the early spring. A good source of information on golf camps is The Guide to Golf Schools and Camps, by Shawguides, Inc., 625 Biltmore Way, Ste. 1408, Coral Gables, FL 33134, (305) 446-8888. Camps usually last from two or three days to a full week, and costs range from as low as $40 per day to $300.

Junior Tournaments

After a series of lessons and a week at golf camp, your child may be ready for competition. Some level of competitive play can heighten interest in the game, and give your child a goal towards which to work.

Before entering a tournament, your child should be hitting the ball with consistency and have a working knowledge of the rules. He should be familiar with principles of golf etiquette and know how to keep score.

Your child's first tournament should be a fun and non-threatening event. If the competition is too intense, it can turn a child off the game. Make sure that your child is really interested in participating, and help him or her to set a realistic goal. Too much emphasis on winning can be destructive. Let him know you want him to play his best and, most of all, have a good time!

Yardstick

The number of yards to the green will usually be indicated on each hole you play, with the exception of par-three holes. This distance is marked by a stake or bush, and often by a cement marker in the center of the fairway.

The marker shows you that it is a measured 150 yards from that location to the center of the green. Note that the measurement does not give you the precise yardage to the flagstick or pin, as it is called, for this position is changed on a daily basis on most courses. (On some courses, the yardage markers give the distance to the front of the green.)

To know the distance to the hole, you can generally be guided either by the color of the flag. Remember: red is closest to the near edge of the green; white indicates center of the green, and blue means the pin is towards the rear. On some courses, the location of the hole is indicated by a plastic ball fixed on the pin. The lower the ball, the closer the hole is to the near edge of the green. You may also play a course which does not offer any clues; in these cases you must rely on your own judgement.

As a beginner, you should start here and now to learn the average distance you strike each club. Because the three wood is the longest fairway club in your bag, it is most likely that you will be hitting a three wood from the fairway position. It is, however, unlikely that you will reach the green with the three wood. Don't worry — you will soon be hitting the green with this club with regularity. That will come with time and practice.

For the sake of this example, we will assume you hit your three wood 150 yards. Below is a chart showing the average distance a beginner will hit each club. For club selection, remember: descending order of distance, ascending number on club.

Average Distances for a Beginner

Club	Yardage	Date	Date	Date	Date	Date
Driver	170					
3 wood	140					
4 wood	130					
3 iron	130					
4 iron	120					
5 iron	110					
6 iron	100					
7 iron	90					
8 iron	80					
9 iron	70					
wedge	60					

As a beginner, you may hit a bit longer or shorter. At this stage in your game, don't worry too much about distance. It is both beneficial and fun, however, to periodically check your distances with the various clubs. The graph on the previous page can be used to record the date and distance you hit the individual clubs as you work on your game. In this way, you will quickly note the improvement you are making!

Here's another handy chart:

Drives in Fairway	Date	Date	Date	Date	Date	No. out of a possible 18
Greens hit in regulation						Par 3-1 stroke Par 4-2 strokes Par 5-3 strokes
Number of putts						Count and enter totals here
Bunker Shots						Enter shots from bunker followed by only one putt

It's easy to note these on a score card. Then enter the information on the chart above and monitor your progress!

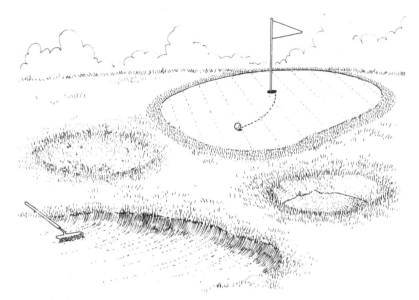

Bunkers and Greens

Observe the average golfer on the practice range, and you often see someone seemingly obsessed with the tee shot. While the drive is an important stroke and often sets the tone for the hole, it is more often the short game that is the determining factor in the total score. For this reason, some special attention should be directed at play from bunkers and around and on the green.

Bunkers

Along with water and marsh, bunkers are a golfer's bug-a-boo. Just about every golf hole you play is going to throw some bunkers at you.

While you are still on the tee box, you should note the location, size, and type of bunkers, and then plot your course to the green where they would have the least opportunity to cause distress.

There are green-side bunkers and fairway bunkers. Bunkers are also called "sand traps," "litter boxes," "beaches," and many more imaginative and unprintable names.

Greens

Having mentioned previously the importance of practicing putting and chipping, let's check the locale where these activities take place, popularly known as: the Green, the Dance Floor, the Short Grass, the Putting Surface.

Now the green can take many shapes besides round. Greens present themselves in a variety of configurations, from kidney-shaped to large, aquatic, and amoebic designs. They can be behind water, or ponds, or streams, as in the famous number twelve hole at Augusta National. Most often, however, you will find the green surrounded with a variety of traps or bunkers .

Once on the green, you must putt. You can also putt from the short grass adjacent to the green. Arnold Palmer once said, "Putt where possible. Your worst putt is often better than your best chip."

When you reach the short grass, you will see players doing what is called, "lining up" their putts. They are calculating the answers to some of the following questions:

- Will the ball run true as it is struck?
- If the green slopes, then in what direction and to what degree? Will the ball "break" to the right or the left?
- If wind is a factor, how will it affect the rolling ball? (Wind can influence the path of a rolling ball in a manner similar to that of a ball in the air.)
- How might the grain (direction in which the blades of grass are growing) affect the roll of the ball?

Greens are not flat like pool tables. There are hills, valleys, and sharp undulations. Putting is often called "the game within the game." The club is different, the swing is different, and it is played on a smooth surface. In putting, you try to consider the variables in as short a time as possible and arrive at a sense of the direction in which to hit the ball and the amount of force to use.

Prior to putting, should you be closer to the hole than your playing group, then mark your ball. This is done by placing a coin or small marker to the rear of the ball (away from the hole). The ball may be cleaned and then replaced when it is your turn to putt. Any debris, leaves, etc., which lie between your ball and the hole may be removed.

In sum:

When you are on the green:

- Be quiet.
- Putt in turn (the player farthest from the hole putts first).
- Make sure your shadow does not cover another player's line.
- Tend the flag if your lie is closest to the hole.
- Repair ball marks, yours and one other.
- When the last putt drops, replace the flag and exit quickly to the following tee.

A Few Famous Places

Augusta, GA
Merion, PA
Harbour Town, SC
Cypress Point, CA
Pine Valley, NJ
Colonial, TX

Firestone, OH
Pinehurst No. 2, NC
Oakmont, PA
Seminole, FL
Torre Pines, CA
Cherry Hill, CO

Listed above are only twelve of the many great courses here in the States. Once you start playing seriously, as surely as every other fanatic, you will find yourself glued to watching the tournaments which are featured on TV: the PGA, the U.S. Open, the Masters, and the many others here and abroad. The Ryder Cup, which is played every two years between European and American players, is one of the best.

TV coverage of golf has greatly improved in the last decade, covering every hole with knowledgeable commentary. Pro play on Saturday and Sunday afternoons during the season are often viewed better on TV from home than from the actual course due to the large crowds which attend the major tournaments.

Four Notables

There is much history and legend behind the creation of all great golf courses. Below are four which are standouts.

Augusta

Atlantan Bobby Jones, a golfing legend in his own right, was instrumental in the creation of the idyllic course known as the Augusta National. After completing his Grand Slam victory in 1930, he retired from competition and turned his attention to transforming a one-time nursery into what is probably the most famous golf course in the world.

The property had been owned by the family of a Belgian Baron, whose son, Prosper Berckmans, became a world renowned horticulturist. His catalog listed 1,300 varieties of pears and 900 different apples among many other fruits, shrubs, and flowers. It has been said that America might not have a single blossoming azalea bush had it not been for the work of Prosper Berckmans.

The course was designed by Scottish architect Dr. Alister Mackenzie, and the Club, designed by Jones, opened in 1932. Two years later, top golfers from around the world were invited to the First Annual Invitation Tournament. This first competitive event was called "a gathering of the masters," and the "Masters" tournament subsequently became one of the major golfing events of the year.

When the Masters is played in early April, the course is ablaze with the colors of blooming dogwoods, azaleas, and other heirs to Berckman's talents. In fact, each hole is named after one of the many shrubs, flowers, or trees on the course.

Among the many famous holes at Augusta National are the eleventh, twelfth, and thirteenth holes, collectively known as "Amen Corner." The name was bestowed by golf writer Herb Warren, who was convinced that prayer was a prerequisite to playing them successfully. Watching the Masters on television confirms that, even today, completing these holes in par makes one most heartily thankful!

Cypress Point

South of San Francisco on the Monterey Peninsula is this magnificent layout. Though not a long course (6,464 yards), it is most difficult to play. The stunning beauty of the holes along the Pacific as well as the forest holes make for indescribably beautiful terrain. Joe Dey, former executive director of the U.S. Golf Association, said that if he were condemned to play only one golf course for the rest of his life, he would pick Cypress Point!

The course was conceived in 1926 by Marion Hollins, the 1921 women's national amateur champion. She, along with Roger Lapham, president of the USGA executive committee, bought the property from the Delmonte Corporation and commissioned Alexander Mackenzie, later associated with the Augusta National, to design the course.

The Cypress Point Club, which opened in 1928, gives new meaning to the term, exclusive. Non-members are not permitted in the clubhouse. For years, even the pros had to change their shoes outside! The use of golf carts is discouraged, and the caddies are reputed to be the best in the world. The Club is devoted only to golf; there are no pools, tennis courts, or other facilities. Among the many notable holes is the sixteenth — a 230-yard par three with all carry over water. Professional golfer Jimmy Demaret said about this hole, "If you miss, your closest drop site is Hawaii."

Pinehurst No. 2

In the piney woods of North Carolina is a Donald Ross gem created in 1907. A "sleeper" among courses, its individual holes are seldom discussed. Pinehurst No. 2 is a player's course, and was a great favorite of Sam Snead and Ben Hogan.

It is also considered by many to be the masterpiece of the great golf course designer, Donald Ross. In golfing you will hear this gentleman's name mentioned often when it comes to course design. Ross was a Scotsman who designed over 500 courses here in the States at the beginning of this century. A favorite theme on a Ross course is the liberal use of sand, and the sandhills of North Carolina offered a perfect site on which he could exercise his talent. Until 1934, all the greens were made of sand, and their surfaces were watered and swept before players putted.

Among hallmarks of the Ross design, which are seen at Pinehurst No. 2, are contoured greens, which resemble the Scottish seaside courses of his native country. Ross built his fairways wide, allowing players a margin of error on their tee shots, but the approach shots call for a degree of accuracy and skill which is challenging to the best golfers.

Here in the U.S. there are Donald Ross courses from Michigan to Florida. Do not, under any circumstance, miss an opportunity to play one. Many golfers have made a pilgrimage through the country playing Ross courses. Pinehurst in the sand hills is a necessary stop.

Merion

Short, tight, and treacherous best describes this mainline Philadelphia layout. Featuring some of the fastest bent grass greens you will ever see, Merion has been the site of many championship tournaments. At 6,544 yards, Merion is a short course by any standard, and it is built on only 126 acres.

The 140 large, white bunkers, known as the White Faces of Merion, appear to be everywhere. The greens are small, tight, and slick. This makes for a most challenging course, and has often humbled some of the biggest names in the sport.

It was at Merion where Bobby Jones competed in his first tournament at the age of 14. At Merion he won the first of his five U.S. Amateur titles, and it was the site of his Grand Slam climax in 1930.

Steeped in tradition, the flagsticks at Merion are still topped by wicker baskets rather than by flags. These are said to be a tribute to the legendary Scottish shepherd said to have invented the game of golf. It was his habit during his noon hour to shoot a ball towards his staff, on the top of which he had hung his lunch basket. For years, the shepherd's lunch baskets were handmade by a town craftsman; today, however, they are "Made in Taiwan!" One of the hallmarks of the Merion course, the baskets, unlike flags, do not reveal the direction of the wind on the green.

St. Andrews

The Royal and Ancient

Golf history dictates that a separate chapter be devoted to this Scottish links masterpiece. If all the history and development of the game could be covered by just one course, it would be this one — the Old Course of the Society of St. Andrews Golfers.

It came into existence on May 14, 1794, at a meeting of 22 noblemen, who enjoyed the game. Since 1834, when King William IV issued the charter which formed the Royal and Ancient Golf Club of St. Andrews, it has been the arbitrator of the game's rules for most of the world, except in America, where the U.S. Golf Association has that responsibility.

Today we recognize the names of famous course architects such as Robert Trent Jones, Pete Dye, and the noted Donald Ross. But if anyone designed St. Andrews, it must have been the Almighty himself.

In the mid-sixteenth century, locals raised rabbits in this open, almost treeless expanse of rolling terrain. By royal decree, farmers were prohibited from cultivating the land; thus humans contributed very little to the development of St. Andrews. The notorious deep bunkers were originally created by sheep, who burrowed deep into the earth during the bitter winter weather.

St. Andrews is situated on the northeast coast by the Bay of Fife, and the winds, whipping through from all directions, can turn it into six different courses within a single round. The ground also can turn stone hard, producing a formidable challenge to the most experienced golfer. Nowhere are distances displayed as they are on courses here in the States; however, such markers would be of little use since the holes extend and shrink according to the direction of the awesome winds.

In addition to the hazards presented by the wind and the bunkers, there are burns, the Scottish term for streams. One noted one is the Swilcan Burn which winds across the fairway and guards the first green.

St. Andrews is a typical links course and originally consisted of 22 holes. As was the custom in that day, golfers played 11 holes out, then turned around and played them back. By 1764, the course was reduced to 18 holes, but only four have their own greens. In fact, the vast double greens are one of St. Andrews' trademarks, requirint 100-foot putts over undulating surfaces.

Another distinctive feature is that the holes all have names such as Hole O'Cross, Cartgate, Ginger Beer, and the noted Road Hole. Most of the famous bunkers have names as well and include Coffins, Cat's Trap, and the dreaded Hell Bunker.

The 14th hole, appropriately named "Long," is a par five with four sets of bunkers, a few of which are so deep that even on tiptoe, you can fail to see the top of the flagstick. Witness Jack Nicklaus himself in the 1995 British Open, swinging again and again to extricate himself from one of St. Andrews' famous bunkers only to finish with an embarrassing score of 10!

St. Andrews has humbled the greatest players in golf, and has proved to be the training ground for many of the world's most outstanding course architects. Of St. Andrews, the great course designer Bobby Trent Jones said, "The more I studied it, the more I loved it."

The Tour and the Tube

"The very magnetic volatility which is the charm of our sisters and our cousins and our aunts, which makes them a delight to the eye and a refreshment to the soul of man, is a heavy handicap when the physical battle and nervous tension waxes long and fierce."
Charles Turner, 1899

Without question, the writer of the words above, which described the American Women's Championship of 1899, would be dismayed were he to tune in one of the many LPGA Tournaments televised regularly on national TV.

A listing of the prominent LPGA competitive events and their approximate schedule follows.

Date	Tournament	Purse
February	Healthsouth Palm Beach Classic	$400,000
	Hawaiian Ladies Open	$500,000

March	Chrysler Plymouth	
	Tournament of Champions	$700,000
	Ping/Welch's Championship	$425,000
	Standard Register Ping	$700,000
	Nabisco Dinah Shore	$700,000
April	Atlanta Women's Championship	$650,000
	Spring Championship	$1,200,000
May	Sara Lee Classic	$525,000
	McDonald's LPGA Championship	$1,100,000
	Lady Keystone Open	$400,000
	LPGA Corning Classic	$500,000
	JC Penney/LPGA Skins Game	$450,000
June	Oldsmobile Classic	$600,000
	Minnesota LPGA Classic	$500,000
	Rochester International	$500,000
	ShopRite LPGA Classic	$500,000
July	Youngstown Warren LPGA Classic	$550,000
	Jamie Farr Toledo Classic	$475,000
	JAL Big Apple Classic	$650,000
	U.S. Women's Open	$800,000
	Ping/Welch's Championship	$450,000
August	McCall's LPGA Classic	
	at Stratton Mountain	$500,000
	Weetabix Women's British Open	$500,000
	Dayton LPGA Classic	$350,000
	Chicago Challenge	$500,000
	duMaurier Ltd. Classic	$800,000
September	State Farm Rail Classic	$525,000
	Ping-Cellular One LPGA Championship	$500,000
	SAFECO Classic	$500,000
	Heartland Classic	$500,000
October	World Championship of Women's Golf	$425,000
	Solhein Cup	
	Nichirei International	$550,000
November	Toray Japan Queens Cup	$700,000
December	JC Penney Classic	$1,200,000

| Diners Club Matches | $500,000 |
| Wendy's Three-Tour challenge | $650,000 |

Such events are not only interesting and enjoyable to watch, they can exert a positive influence on your game. It is inspiring to see a field of skillful professional women golfers. And, it is also instructive.

Here are some things to look for. Choose several players whose physical build matches your own. Focus on the lady pro's technique. Observe her stance, her manner of addressing the ball, and her swing. Take note of the differences in her drive, fairway shots, and short game. Look for an established pre-swing routine. One of the most important elements to examine is her timing.

Unconsciously, while you are watching, your physical reflexes are responding. You can and may imitate what you have seen the next time you play.

The television commentators often have useful information to share, and many televised tournaments include a "tips for golfers" feature which may be helpful.

Famous Ladies of the Links

"I'm going to loosen my girdle and let it rip."
Babe Didrikson Zaharias
1914-1955

The Ladies Professional Golf Association (LPGA) got its start in 1949 when Fred Corcoran, manager for Babe Didrikson Zaharias, was asked to meet with seven of the leading female professional golfers to establish an organization which would promote competition and enhance public awareness of women's golf.

In the first tournament organized by Corcoran, all players finished in the money — even one who never teed off. Helen Dettweiler received $350 even though she was unable to play because her dog was sick!

Needless to say, times and standards have changed. Today, to achieve a place in the LPGA Hall of Fame, one must not only tee off, but win either 30 tournaments, plus two majors; 35

tournaments with one major; or a total of 40 tournaments. The careers of some outstanding women golfers are highlighted below.

Patty Berg

Born in Minneapolis in 1918, Berg took up the game at the age of 12, after quarterbacking the neighborhood all-male football team and distinguishing herself as a speed skater. She won the Minneapolis City Championship at age 15, and over the next seven years, she won 29 tournaments while still an amateur. Turning professional in 1940, she would win 55 tournaments before she retired from competition at the age of 62.

A founder and charter member of the LPGA, she served as the organization's president for the first four years of its existence. She was the first golfer inducted into the LPGA Hall of Fame, and she and Babe Zaharias won 19 of the 23 tournaments they entered during the first two years of the LPGA.

A generous and enthusiastic promoter of the game, Berg is reputed to have conducted more clinics than any other golfer in history, and was the first woman pro to give an exhibition in Japan.

JoAnne Gunderson Carner

At 5' 7", Carner was dubbed "Big Mama," both for her stature and powerful swing. In 1981, she was the fifth woman to earn the U.S. Golf Association's Bob Jones Sportsmanship Award.

Born in Kirkland, Washington, in 1939, Carner won the Girls' Junior Championship as a teenager, and, at age 18, won her first U.S. Amateur Championship, a title she reclaimed in 1960, 1962, 1966, and 1968. She was the youngest player to set such a record since Beatrice Hoyt's outstanding accomplishments in 1896. Carner competed on four different Curtis Cup teams, and was the last amateur to win an LPGA event, the 1969 Burdine's Invitational in Miami.

Turning pro at age 30, she was named Rookie of the Year in 1970. She won the U.S. Open in 1971, and went on to win more official tournaments and collect more Vare trophies than any other player of that time. In 1978, she became the first player to win $100,000 three years running. She was inducted into the LPGA Hall of Fame in 1982.

Glenna Collett Vare

Born in New Haven, Connecticut, in 1903, she is described as the greatest American amateur player. Capable of driving the ball a great distance, at 18 years of age and 5'6" tall, she could hit a tee shot over 300 yards, the longest measured drive hit by a woman. Dominating women's golf during the '20's, in 1929 she lost narrowly to the great British golfer, Joyce Wethered, in the British final at St. Andrews.

In 1935, she advanced to her eighth Women's Amateur final and, beating Patty Berg, she earned her sixth victory. This win ended a 13-year run in the Women's Amateur during which she won six times, finished second twice, and advanced to the quarterfinals or semifinals three times. Not even the great Bobby Jones, who figured in seven U.S. Amateur finals, equalled her domination of this single event.

Babe Didrikson Zaharias

Credited with changing the way women approached the game of golf, Zaharias was a pioneer in women's professional golf and a founder of the LPGA. In her eight-year professional career, she won 31 of the 128 events scheduled.

Born in Port Arthur, Texas, in 1914, she has been voted the greatest female athlete of all time in every poll ever taken. As described by Rhonda Glenn in the *Illustrated History of Women's Golf,* she could "run, jump, throw the javelin and the discus, play tennis, polo, basketball, marbles, soccer, lacrosse, billiards; she could dive, ride, shoot, pitch, bat home runs, kick, fence, pass, bowl, and skate. She was an exquisite ballroom and adagio dancer, played the harmonica well enough to be a professional at it, excelled at gin rummy, was a good cook and a great seamstress, and could type 100 words a minute."

At age 17, Didrikson won six of the seven American Track and Field championship events she entered and set world records in three of them. Qualifying for the 1932 Olympics, she won three events. She chose to concentrate on golf after winning the second tournament she entered.

A natural athlete, she was a powerful golfer and could drive the ball 250 yards off the tee. Assisted with other elements of her game by golfing legends Walter Hagen and Gene Sarazen, she won 17 consecutive amateur tournaments in 1946 and 1947, including both the U.S. Women's championship and the British title. Turning professional in 1948, she won a U.S. Open title, three Women's Titleholder victories, and four Western Open championships in her first year on the tour.

She was the first women to hold the title of head professional at a golf club and was voted by the Associated Press as the Woman Athlete of the Half Century in 1949.

Undergoing cancer surgery in 1953, she astounded an admiring public by coming back to win the U.S. Open title in 1954, finishing 12 strokes better than the second place finisher. She won four other events that year and two more the following year before she succumbed to her illness in 1955.

Nancy Lopez

Born in Torrance, California, in 1957, Nancy Lopez was at the forefront of the transformation of professional women's golf. Since she launched her professional career in 1977, LPGA purses have nearly quadrupled.

Learning golf from her father, she became the New Mexico Women's amateur champion at age 12. She won her first U.S. Golf Association's Junior Girl's title at age 15, and at age 21, her first LPGA tournament. Just nine years later, she was inducted into the LPGA Hall of Fame.

Her first year on the tour, she won $23,138, but she broke all records during her second season. Technically still a rookie in 1978, she won nine of the 25 tournaments she entered, earning $189,813 as well as the LPGA Player and Rookie of the Year awards. The year 1979 saw a repeat performance, and her 71.20 stroke average set an LPGA record.

Instantly and overwhelmingly popular both with the public and the press, Lopez is credited with building a tremendous following for women's golfing events.

In 1982, she married baseball player Ray Knight, and became a tour millionaire in winnings at the 1983 Nabisco-Dinah Shore. In subsequent years, she continued to pile up victories while raising three children. In 1985, she became the first LPGA player to earn over $400,000 in a single season and set another scoring record with an average of 70.73.

Lopez was inducted into the LPGA Hall of Fame in 1987 after winning her 35th official tournament. Still a popular player on the tour, through 1991, Lopez had won 44 tournaments and more than $3 million.

Betsy Rawls

Born in Texas 1928, she was a four-time winner of the U.S. Open and one of the biggest money winners in the history of the LPGA. Although she did not start playing golf until age 17, she was tutored by the now legendary Harvey Penick, and within four years she was good enough to win the Trans-National Amateur and the Texas Women's Amateur titles.

A Phi Beta Kappa graduate in physics from the University of Texas, she turned professional in 1951 and over the next 20 years won more than 50 tournaments and close to a quarter-million dollars in prize money. She retired in 1975 and served for six years as Tournament Director for the LPGA tour. She was the first woman to serve on the rules committee of the U.S. Open, and was elected to the World Golf Hall of Fame.

Louise Suggs

Born in Atlanta in 1923, she first played golf at age 10 and was taught the game by her father, a former professional baseball player. After a successful amateur career, she won 50 tournaments on the Ladies' PGA tour.

Turning professional in 1948, she won the U.S. Open twice and the LPGA championship once. She was twice the tour's leading money winner. In 1953, her best year, she earned $20,000, a considerable sum at that time. In 1960, she became the first women to out play men professionally. Hitting from the same tees, she defeated Sam Snead and a dozen other top male players at the Royal Poinciana Invitational.

Joyce Wethered (Lady Heathcoat-Armory)

Born in England in 1901, she was rated for many years as the greatest female golfer in the history of the game, and was considered the equal of Babe Zaharias and Mickey Wright.

Launching her career in 1920, she was unbeaten for the next five years, winning the English Ladies championship five times and the British Women's championship four times. She retired in 1925, but returned to play and triumph over Glenna Collett at St. Andrews in 1929. Her brother, Roger, was one of Britain's finest amateur players during the same decade.

Kathy Whitworth

The standard against which all professional women golfers are measured, Kathy Whitworth was the first female to reach $1 million in earnings and holds the U.S. record for her 88 official career professional wins, surpassing Sam Snead's grand total of 81.

Born in 1939, in Monahans, Texas, she later attributed her success to having been born in a small town. Whitworth grew to 5'9", and started hitting golf balls in a cow pasture at age 15. She was a devoted pupil of Harvey Penick, sending yellow roses to him after her 83rd win. She won the New Mexico State Amateur title in 1957 and turned professional in 1958.

After a slow start on the tour, Whitworth emerged from the shadow of Mickey Wright, four years her senior, in 1965. That year she won eight tournaments, nine in 1966, eight in 1967, and ten in 1968. She earned a place in the LPGA Hall of Fame in 1975. Over the next ten years, she averaged two tournament victories and $100,000 annually.

Mickey Wright

Born in San Diego, California, in 1935, Mickey Wright stood a powerful 5'9" tall. Winning the U.S. Girls Junior Championship at the age of 17, two years later she was partnered with Babe Zaharias for the final day of the U.S. Open and finished tied for fourth. Inspired by Zaharias and her own strong performance, Wright decided to leave Stanford University and join the LPGA tour in 1955.

One of the longest hitters on the tour, she struggled with her short game, and ultimately became almost unbeatable. In 1958, she won the U.S. Open and the LPGA Championship. The string of victories continued in the early '60's; within nine years, Wright won 79 of her 82 titles, an achievement equalled only by Kathy Whitworth, and averaged nearly eight victories a year. Wright retired in 1971, but not before her swing was described by Ben Hogan as the finest he ever saw.

Last Thoughts
"A Walk in the Park"

Golf is a walk in the park." So says pro golfer Fuzzy Zoeller, echoing and re-phrasing author Mark Twain's famous quip that golf is "a good walk, spoiled!"

Of course, golf is more than that.

It's the smell of the grass, the song of a bird, the flight of a hawk, and the scent of a breeze after its trip through the pines.

It's many good friends and lots of laughs. It's the occasional forty-foot putt that rattles in the cup, and it's the long, soaring drive that splits the fairway.

It's a bad slice that hits a tree and turns up on the short grass. Golf is all these things and more.

The game played on nature's course is a lot of good things, and yours to discover.

References

Campbell, Malcolm. *Random House International Encyclopedia of Golf.* New York: Random, 1991.

Davis, William H. and the Editors of Golf Digest. *Great Golf Courses of the World.* New York: Harper, 1974.

Dennis, Larry. *Beginner's Guide to Golf.* Jupiter, FL: National Golf Foundation, 1994.

Editors of Golf Magazine. *Golf Magazine's Encyclopedia of Golf.* New York: Harper Collins, 1993.

Garber, Angus G. III. *Golf Legends.* Stamford, CT: Michael Friedman Publishing Group, 1988, 1993.

Glenn, Rhonda. *The Illustrated History of Women's Golf.* Dallas, Texas: Taylor Publishing Company, 1991.

Hecker, Genevieve. *Golf for Women.* New York: Baker and Taylor, 1904.

Lopez, Nancy with Peter Schwed. *The Education of a Woman Golfer.* New York: Simon & Schuster, 1979.

Ruthenberg, Stephen. *Golf Fore Beginners: The Fundamentals.* Lansing, Michigan: RGS Publishing, 1992.

Shapiro, Mel; Dohn, Warren; Berger, Leonard. *Golf: A Turn of the Century Treasury.* Secaucus, N.J: Castle, 1986.

Wire, Gary. *The PGA Manual of Golf.* New York: MacMillan, 1991.

Yocum, Lewis A. and Mottram, Robert with Burns, Bill. *Women's Exercise Guide to Better Golf.* Inglewood, California: Champion Press, 1988.